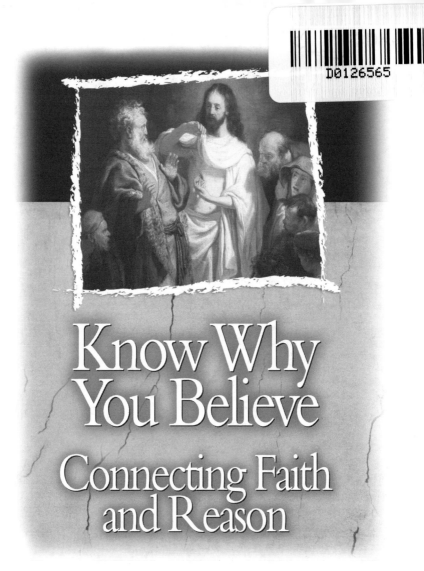

Know Why You Believe

Connecting Faith and Reason

PAUL E. LITTLE

UPDATED AND EXPANDED
BY MARIE LITTLE

Victor®
The Bible Teacher's Teacher

COOK COMMUNICATIONS MINISTRIES
Colorado Springs, Colorado • Paris, Ontario
KINGSWAY COMMUNICATIONS, LTD.
Eastbourne, England

Victor® is an imprint of
Cook Communications Ministries, Colorado Springs, Colorado 80918
Cook Communications, Paris, Ontario
Kingsway Communications, Eastbourne, England

Know Why You Believe
© 2003 by Marie Little, fifth edition
previous ISBN 1-56476-754-X

First printing, 2000
Printed in the United States of America

49 50 51 52 53 54 Printing/Year 10 09 08 07 06

Editor over fifth edition revision: Craig Bubeck, Sr. Editor
Cover design: Image Studios
Front cover image: Christ Showing His Wounds to Saint Thomas, by Rembrandt;
© Archivo Iconografico, S.A./CORBIS

First edition published by Scripture Press Publications, Inc. in 1967; © 1967, 1980, 1987, 1999.

Library of Congress Cataloging-in-Publication Data

Little, Paul E.
  Know why you believe / Paul E. Little.
    p. cm.
  Rev. ed. of: The answer to life. 1987.
  ISBN 0-7814-3963-9 (pbk.)
  1. Apologetics. 2. Christian life. I. Little, Paul E. Title.
  BT1102 .L5 2003
  239--dc21

CONTENTS

INTRODUCTION
How This Book Began

"After 2,000 years, no question is going to bring Christianity crashing."

With cryptic statements like this my husband, Paul, found his niche in university settings talking to students about Christianity.

Paul fearfully approached the designated "Greek" house at the University of Kansas for a 6 p.m. dinner where he would give a fifteen-minute introductory talk followed by questions from the men. As a new staff member with InterVarsity Christian Fellowship, he was terrified. His fears were magnified because it was a scholarship hall—really brainy students. Further, it was a Jewish scholarship hall! He later described his prayer that day as he walked to the door of the fraternity house:

> Lord, you know I always stub my toe when I try to explain
> Christian basics clearly to people with questions. Why must I
> begin in a residence reserved for the smartest students? They'll
> tear me apart limb from limb. I'll not live the night out!

To Paul's amazement, one young man had his life turned around that night by the "new" thought that God offered him a new life and the power to live it. That young man decided to become a Christian.

Encouraged by the good response of this one man, Paul continued. He traveled from campus to campus, leading dorm and fraternity sessions and tirelessly spending hours talking one-on-one with students. From hundreds of campuses on five continents he sought to capture the attention of the bored, the intellectual, the athletic. He used clipped questions to jog the thinking and help the listeners examine their present worldviews, ranging from scientific determinism to rabid existentialism. He sprinkled in a few "sure-fire jokes" and other good humor. He'd say, "You exercised blind faith if you ate in a restaurant today." "Believing something doesn't make it true; refusing to believe it doesn't make it false." "Many people who say they don't believe the Bible have actually never read it."

In twenty-five years of lecturing Paul found that regardless of the group there were twelve commonly asked questions. "They are predictable," he said. "If we think through the answers to the common questions we hear, we'll know the answers to the right ones. Right answers to the wrong questions aren't of much help!" From his own study of the Bible and research of biblical scholars, he framed his answers. That's how *Know Why You Believe* was born.

The message of this newly edited book is entirely Paul's. I have added some new illustrations from the specialized fields of archaeology and science. In each area I have followed the capsulized biblical basics that are Paul's intentional focus. Two scholars and dialecticians from the staff of Willow Creek Community Church, Judson Poling and Brad Mitchell, have provided me with indispensible help in preparing this edition. I am indebted to both for their wisdom.

It has been decades since the day when the dread news came of my husband's death in an automobile accident. I am awed that God has continued using these answers. Paul would probably shake his head soberly and say, "This is God's work; the light comes from him." The Bible is stalwart and trustworthy in the light of any challenge. As Paul said, no one will think up a question that will bring Christianity crashing even after two thousand years. The many stories I continue to hear of God's using these words affirm the extraordinary impact of God's truth that we all seek.

Just recently I gave a copy of this book to a searching young Sikh woman. After she and her husband had visited me several times in my living room she told me, "This book answered all my questions." She became a fully devoted follower of Jesus Christ— additionally, a sterling wife and mother. Amazing grace.

Marie Little
Mt. Prospect, Illinois

CHAPTER ONE

IS CHRISTIANITY RATIONAL?

"What is faith?" asked the Sunday School teacher. A young boy answered in a flash, "Believing something you know isn't true."

It's not surprising that many investigating faith and Christianity define it this way. In reality, many Christians overtly or secretly also hold this view. For twenty-five years I've been asking this question in college and university discussions across the country. The average student of higher education might give the same answer as the boy. It may be couched in different terms, but the idea of self-deception and unreliability is usually there.

In these student sessions I describe in simple terms the definition of faith given in the Bible. Then I ask for questions from the floor. The responses are eye-opening.

DON'T KISS YOUR BRAINS GOODBYE

Seekers will quizzically remark that the sessions have been helpful because for the first time they have heard a down-to-earth, concise summation of the Christian message. The convinced Christians at times say they are relieved to hear the Christian story coherently defended in the open marketplace of ideas. They see they haven't kissed their brains goodbye in becoming believers!

We live in an increasingly sophisticated and educated world where new choices compete for our attention. Unknowingly, our certainties become diluted with attractive indulgences and our belief systems wobble. This kind of world heightens our need to know *why* we believe and examine the truths to support that belief. What truths do we live by?

On the important question of whether Christianity is rational and can withstand scrutiny, we begin with the widely misunderstood word *faith*. Three thoughts come to mind.

We all use faith every day. It is quite impossible to avoid using faith—even setting aside religious faith. We have faith in the doctor, faith in the grocery store, faith in the person who asks us for a date. We even have faith that the train will arrive to take us to work or that the mail carrier will bring our paycheck. The scientist has faith in the scientific method learned from previous scientists, assuming they were honest. Faith then is simply trust; we must exercise at least some measure of faith in order to interact meaningfully with the real world.

Faith is only as valid as the object in which it is placed. Trust an untested food, an unqualified doctor or a dishonest person, and the faith is not valid. A sad example of misplaced faith is the story of a young student who told me that his girlfriend had long been dating another man and would soon marry him. Faith may be well intentioned but the object unproven, rendering the faith useless. Meager faith placed in a reliable object, however, will bring results. For instance, if you have weak faith in thick ice, the result is nonetheless positive: the ice holds your weight regardless of your strength of faith.

No opinion poll is going to make God go away.

Testing the reliability of objects of faith is rational and certainly advisable. Wisdom leads us to investigate and know the true facts of any object of our faith. If a clock is wrong, we adjust it. It's the sensible thing to do.[1]

EXAMINE OUR PRIOR THINKING

These few examples of faith help us see it as a normal part of our lives. From there we turn to examine as objectively as possible the rationality of the Christian faith. Objectivity is inevitably colored by *our prior thinking* about Christianity. What facts do we know about it? Do we view it as rational or irrational? Relevant or irrelevant? In those student sessions their prior thinking was glaringly obvious by the questions they asked. Some questions had to do largely with lack of information, others with misunderstandings of the basic content of

Christianity. There were always penetrating questions and "why" enigmas brought with deep earnestness.

One's prior thinking is a key factor. "What you think you know can hurt you" was the title of an article in the *Chicago Tribune*. "A little knowledge can turn out to be harmful to your financial health" was the subtitle, listing fifteen or more examples of befuddled thinking common to investors, like "I try to save money by going to the store every time there's a sale." Too little knowledge of what the Christian faith is all about might also be harmful. In what areas have we been crystal clear about true Christianity and where have we been befuddled in our thinking?

Another cloud to faith, in addition to our prior thinking, is our "emotional quotient" or E.Q., as it is called. Whether our heritage is the United States or some other country, there may have been both erroneous or obnoxious examples of practicing Christians who have turned us off. Our E.Q. may go through the roof if we even hear the word "Christian." Granted, we all have emotional hang-ups of some kind, but awareness of them does help. On the other hand, we may have had zero contacts with Christians or Christianity, no information and no hang-ups. In either case, the more we can comprehend our own origins of thinking and feeling, the more objectively we will be able to consider the "case for Christianity," as C. S. Lewis put it.

Biblical Christianity has very specific, comprehensible bases. It is not an esoteric religion. Its content is not concealed in vague symbols, says scholar R. C. Sproul. When someone tells you in a hushed whisper that the meaning to life is "one hand clapping," that's esoteric, according to Sproul. This is not what we know as a rational basis for thinking. Certainly it is not the idea we intend to convey by "rational thinking."[2]

Any number of religions might claim spiritual experiences that may approximate ours. From the time of nineteenth-century philosopher Friedrich Neitzsche to today, from outside Christendom to within, we are being told God is dead. Ethical humanism is having stronger appeal. Julian Huxley's *Religion Without Revelation* is a good example of the approach that claims God is dead. Pluralism has taken over with modern communications in making the world a neighborhood. We are likely to hear:

1. All religions are equally valid.
2. Contradictions between religious systems are fully acceptable.
3. Absolute truth does not exist.

9

CHRISTIANITY TESTED OBJECTIVELY?

Analytical philosopher Antony Flew states that to the person who is searching, religious assertions *incapable of being tested objectively* are meaningless. He illustrates from a graphic tale told by John Wisdom:

> Once upon a time two explorers came upon a clearing in the jungle. In the clearing were growing many flowers and many weeds. One explorer says, "Some gardener must tend this plot." The other disagrees, "There is no gardener." So they pitch their tents and set a watch. No gardener is ever seen. "But perhaps he is an invisible gardener." So they set up a barbed wire fence. They electrify it. They patrol with bloodhounds. (For they remember how H. G. Wells' *The Invisible Man* could be both smelled and touched though he could not be seen.) But no shrieks ever suggest that some intruder has received a shock. No movements of the wire ever betray an invisible climber. The bloodhounds never give cry. Yet still the believer is not convinced. "But there is a gardener, invisible, insensible to electric shocks, a gardener who comes secretly to look after the garden which he loves." At last the skeptic despairs, "But what remains of your original assertion? Just how does what you call an invisible, intangible, eternally elusive gardener differ from an imaginary gardener or even from no gardener at all?"[3]

Evangelical scholar John Montgomery comments on the story. "In Christianity we do not have merely an allegation that the garden of this world is tended by a loving Gardener; we have the actual, *empirical entrance* of the Gardener into the human scene in the person of Jesus Christ (John 20:14-15), and this entrance is verifiable by way of his resurrection."[4]

A RATIONAL BODY OF TRUTH

Too often the Christian faith is not considered seriously, merely looked upon as one of a number of truth claims and not seen as built on any verifiable truth. Faith and superstition look like partners.

However the opposite is true. The Bible itself stresses the importance of revealed rational processes. Jesus stressed this to his disciples, "Love the Lord your God with all your heart . . . and with all your

10

mind" (Matthew 22:37). The whole person is involved in putting our faith in him: the mind, the emotions and the will. The apostle Paul described himself as "defending and confirming the gospel," for example, giving an apologetic for his faith (Philippians 1:7). All of this implies a clearly understandable message that can be rationally understood and supported.

Belief doesn't create truth. Unbelief doesn't destroy truth.

An unenlightened mind is one never exposed to the truth of God, but enlightenment brings satisfying comprehension when based on a rational body of truth. Every one of us from childhood to adulthood needs reasons and explanations. Tell a child he'll get burned if he touches a hot grill. Only then can he make the choice to touch or not touch. But he has been enlightened. So it is for us. Enlightenment comes from knowledge of the primary Christian truths.

Christian faith goes *beyond* reason but not *against* reason.

The Christian faith is always equated with truth. And truth is always the opposite of error (2 Thessalonians 2:11-12). People who have not yet believed are called by Paul as those who "reject the truth" (Romans 2:8). It follows that these statements would be meaningless unless there were a way to establish truth objectively. If there were no such possibility, truth and error would, for all practical purposes, be the same. The root question is, does absolute truth exist? One clear evidence is given us.

CREATION MAKES IT PLAIN

Creation itself, the apostle Paul states logically, gives all people enough knowledge to know there is a God. In Romans 1:19 he states, "God has made it plain to them." God is easy for anyone to see; he is not hidden. Paul then tells us to look at the creation. "For since the creation of the world God's invisible qualities . . . have been clearly seen." He goes on to say God's two major qualities are equally evident, *"His eternal power and divine nature"* (Romans 1:20, emphasis added).

From this small, yet potent, verse it is explained that God expects us to believe in him based on comprehensible evidence. He gives us intelligent and logical reasons. He is saying, "Look at the natural world,

11

even the universe or your own body and you will have ample evidence for belief in a Creator." The "handiwork," the uncommon masterpiece of the divine Creator, tells us of his meticulous care and sustaining activity in his creation.

His *"eternal power"* is not an easy phrase to wrap our thinking around. Bill Hybels gives us a glimpse.

> God knows everything. No questions can confound Him . . . but this knowledge extends even farther than today's events. God knows how all things work. Think about that. He has all the complete knowledge of all of the mysteries of biology, physiology, zoology, chemistry, psychology, geology, physics, medicine and genetics. He knows the ordinances of heaven, as well as the reasons and course for the sun and the moon and the clouds.[5]

We could say this gives a definition of *infinite*, not *finite* as we are. Furthermore, God knows the big picture of every facet of our personal lives.

SEEING THE BIG PICTURE

This fact heightens our incentive to explore some answers to how we fit into "the big picture" from God's horizon. Why are we here, living in this family and at this place? Does it matter what choices we make and what we do each day? How did we happen to be in this country and not some other? What will happen when we leave this life?

Volumes have been written on the "why" of our existence, hence it is not a new question. It is something we all ask at some time or other. In his bestselling book *A Brief History of Time,* Stephen Hawking sums up his lifetime of research and thinking by asking one question. After concluding his ideas on the "what" and the "how" of the universe, he says (seemingly with longing), "Now if we only knew the why, we would have the mind of God."[6]

Could it be such personal "heart" questions, or may it be a sense of emptiness and loss that provokes such questions from many? One longtime movie actress aptly described it as a "hole in the soul" that started her seeking. The essence of God's picture for us in the Bible is to give us the answers. We need not stay in the dark. There is every evidence God wants us to know the answers.

C. S. Lewis explains, "It is easy to say we believe a rope to be strong and sound as long as we are merely using it to wrap a box. But suppose you had to hang by that rope over a precipice. You would really want to first discover how trustworthy that rope was."[7]

MORAL SMOKE SCREENS

Our understanding can be unknowingly hindered by moral smoke screens, overshadowing the intellectual revelation of God and darkening our understanding. The moral pull can be intractable, insatiable, unwilling to go away. In some cases, the true issue is not that people cannot believe—it is that they "will not believe." Jesus was straightforward about this as the root of the problem when talking to the highly religious Pharisees, the legalistic rulers of his day. "You refuse to come to me," he told them, "to have life" (John 5:40). Jesus then goes on to say that when a moral commitment is made, it brings understanding to the mind. It even brings resolution to intellectual roadblocks. "If anyone chooses to do God's will, he will find out whether my teaching comes from God or whether I speak on my own" (John 7:17).

Alleged intellectual problems are often a smoke screen covering moral rebellion. As the poet Emily Dickinson put it, "Fail in an instant, no man did. Slipping—is Crash's law."

Another digression I've heard is, "If Christianity is rational and true, why is it that most educated people don't believe it?" The answer is simple. They don't believe it for the same reason that most uneducated people don't believe it. They don't want to believe it. It's not a matter of brain power, for there are outstanding Christians in every field of the arts and sciences. Belief is ultimately a matter of the will. And God has given us starting evidence with creation.

> If morality is only "feeling derived," *who makes the rules?* If Christianity is only "feeling derived," it leads to absurdity. Faith involves mind and heart.

13

A student once told me I had satisfactorily answered all his questions. "Are you going to become a Christian?" I asked.

"No," he replied.

Puzzled, I asked, "Why not?"

He admitted, "Frankly, because it would mess up the way I'm living." He realized the real issue for him was not intellectual but moral.

John Stott struck a balance when he summarized how to explain the Christian story: "We cannot pander to a man's intellectual arrogance, but we must cater to his intellectual integrity."

DOUBT STRIKES TERROR

Even committed Christians question their faith and wonder if it's true. Doubt can strike terror to the soul and be suppressed in an unhealthy way. Those who have grown up in Christian homes and in the Christian church find it easy to doubt the authenticity of their early experiences. From their youth they have accepted the facts of Christianity solely on the basis of confidence and trust in parents, friends and pastor. As the educational process develops, there is a reexamination of how much of their early teaching they own for themselves.

Such an experience is healthy and necessary to make our faith virile and genuine. It's nothing to fear or to be shocked about. At times when I travel to new places, I tend to ask myself, looking at unfamiliar streets and people, "Little, how do you know you haven't been taken in by a colossal propaganda program? After all, you can't see God, touch him, taste him or feel him." And then I go on to ask myself how I know the God and Jesus Christ of the Bible is true. I always come back to two basic factors:

1. the objective, external, historical facts of the resurrection

2. the subjective, internal, personal experience of Jesus Christ that I have known in my own life through serious surgery and hard career decisions

When a person, young or old, begins to question and God seems far away, doubts should be welcomed as a way to grow. A Christian can help by welcoming the honesty and openness, creating a climate where a person feels free to "unload" and express doubts. If not, a person can be driven underground, even turned away by someone with a high shock index, implying that a good Christian would never doubt. The questioner feels judged harshly. They aren't stupid. Sadly, I've seen some who have met an unloving

Does the human spirit need faith in God?

• Does a car run on soda water?

• Does a tree need roots?

• Does your soul feel empty?

response, quickly shift gears and mouth the party line. But it doesn't genuinely come from the heart. When they are out from under pressure to conform, they shed their faith like a raincoat because it has never become their very own.

Doubt and questioning are normal to any thinking person. Rather than express shock, listen to the questioner and, if possible, even sharpen the question further. Then an answer can be suggested. Unflinchingly we can discuss problems, because Christianity centers on the One who is Truth, and scrutiny is no threat.

DON'T HIT THE PANIC BUTTON

For any of us, if we don't find an answer to a question immediately, we needn't hit the panic button. We can keep searching, crystallize the question and check out books specializing on seemingly unsolvable questions. It is improbable that anyone thought up, last week, a question that will bring Christianity crashing. Brilliant minds have probed through the profound questions of every age and have ably answered them.

Full answers to every possible question may allude us. We are not God! He hasn't fully revealed his mind to us on every conceivable query. "The secret things belong to the LORD our God, but the things revealed belong to us and to our children forever" (Deuteronomy 29:29). This is not a cop out! God gives us more than enough information, however, to have a solid foundation under our faith and life. Christianity is based on *reasonable* faith.

If the thought of checking out a mountain of evidence overwhelms you, don't panic. In the college and university setting the audience may be composed of 98 percent agnostics. After a while, it became possible to predict the questions that would generally be asked in the course of a half-hour question period. The questions may vary in wording, but the underlying issues were the same. This consistency was a great help to know the major questions and where to sharpen my own knowledge, and how to shape the thoughts in this book.

A DOUBTER'S RESPONSE

Doubters have been known to see where troubling issues lie. After hearing answers to their questions, a decision is the next step. To make no decision is to decide against the Christian position. Continued doubt in the face of adequate information means not to give up but to keep seeking and eventually you will be rewarded. "Christianity is not a patent medicine. It claims to give an account of facts—to tell you what the real universe is like. If Christianity is untrue, then no honest person will want to believe it. However, if it is true, every honest person will want to believe it. . . . All right, Christianity will do you good—a great deal more good than you ever expected!"[8]

We can be assured our genuine seeking will be rewarded. In the following pages we shall spotlight some answers to the commonly asked questions and get the facts straight. You can believe it, for Christianity is true and rational. Jesus gave us this encouragement: "I have come that [you] may have life, and have it to the full" (John 10:10).

FOR FURTHER READING

Clark, Kelly James. *Philosophers Who Believe.* Downers Grove, Ill.: InterVarsity Press, 1993.

Johnson, Phillip E. *Reason in the Balance.* Downers Grove, Ill.: InterVarsity Press, 1995.

———. *Objections Sustained.* Downers Grove, Ill.: InterVarsity Press, 1998.

CHAPTER TWO

IS THERE A GOD?

In human existence there is no more profound question demanding an answer. *Is there a God?* is a question that challenges every thinking person, and the answer has far-reaching implications for each of us no matter where we are in life.

While we were living in Dallas, a salesman of *Great Books of the Western World* convinced us to buy the fifty-four volume set. Of its 102 great ideas, I began with number twenty-nine, *God*. The editor, Mortimer Adler, begins with the explanation: "In sheer quantity of references, as well as in variety, this is the largest chapter [of the introductory syntopicon]. The reason is obvious. More consequences for thought and action follow the affirmation or denial of God than from answering any other basic question."

Adler goes on to spell out the practical implications: the whole tenor of human life is affected by whether people regard themselves as supreme beings in the universe or acknowledge a superhuman being whom they conceive of as an object of fear or love, a force to be defied or a Lord to be obeyed. Among those who acknowledge a divinity, it matters greatly whether the divine is represented merely by the concept of God—the object of philosophical speculation—or by the living God whom people worship in all the acts of piety which comprise the rituals of religion.[1]

GOD IN A TEST TUBE?

It is obvious we cannot examine God in a test tube or prove him by the usual scientific methodology. Furthermore, we can say with equal emphasis that it is not possible to prove Napoleon by the scientific method. The reason lies in the nature of history itself and in the limitations of the scientific method. In order for something to be proved by the scientific method, it must be repeatable. A scientist does not announce a new finding to the world on the basis of a single experiment. History in its very nature is nonrepeatable. No one can rerun the beginning of the universe or bring Napoleon back or repeat the assassination of Lincoln or the crucifixion of Jesus Christ. *The fact that these events can't be proved by repetition does not disprove their reality as events.*

There are many real things outside the scope of verification by the scientific method. The scientific method is useful only with measurable, material things. No one has ever seen three feet of love or two pounds of justice, but one would be foolish indeed to deny their reality. To insist that God be proved by the scientific method is like insisting that a telephone be used to measure radioactivity.

ETERNITY IN OUR HEARTS

What evidence is there for God? Anthropological research has indicated there is a universal belief in God among the most remote peoples today. In the earliest histories and legends of peoples all around the world the original concept was of *one* God, who is the Creator. An original *high God* appears to have been in their consciousness even in those societies that are today polytheistic. Regardless of other accretions added to this unknown god, the idea of one God has persisted.

Research in the last fifty years has challenged the evolutionary concept of religion's development. Monotheism—the concept of one God—became the apex of a gradual development that began with polytheistic concepts. It is increasingly clear that the oldest traditions everywhere were of one supreme God.[2] The writer of Ecclesiastes referred to God as having "set eternity in the hearts of men" (3:11).

Blaise Pascal, the great seventeenth-century mathematician, wrote of "the God-shaped vacuum" in every person. Augustine concluded, "Our hearts are restless until they rest in thee."

The evidence shows that the vast majority of humanity, at all times and in all places, has believed in some kind of god or gods. Though this fact is not conclusive proof by any means, it is a beginning reference point to keep in mind as we attempt to answer the big question.

LAW OF CAUSE AND EFFECT

The basic question is not whether God *exists* but whether God is *good!*

Consider the law of cause and effect. No effect can be produced without a cause. There's a note in your door. Someone put it there. The painting on the wall, someone drew it. Nothing comes from nothing! We as human beings and the universe itself are effects that must have had a cause. We come eventually to an uncaused cause, who is God.

The noted skeptic Bertrand Russell makes an astounding statement in his *Why I Am Not a Christian*. He says that when he was a child, "God" was given him as the answer to the many questions he raised about existence. In desperation he asked, "Well, who created God?" When no answer was forthcoming, he says, "My entire faith collapsed." Unfortunately, his is a common experience, yet it fails to answer the burning question.

"An eternal God is outside of time, but knowable."

Hugh Ross

God, the Creator, the Beginner, by definition is eternal. He is uncreated. He is self-existent. Were God a created being, he would not be a cause, he would be an effect. He would not and could not be God.

R. C. Sproul explains, "Being eternal, God is not an effect. Since he is not an effect, he does not *require* a cause. He is uncaused. It is important to note the difference between an uncaused, self-existent eternal being and an effect that causes itself through self-creation."[3]

INFINITE TIME PLUS CHANCE?

No one would think a computer could come into being without an intelligent designer. It is unlikely that a monkey in a print shop could set Lincoln's Gettysburg Address in type. If we found a copy of it, we would conclude that an intelligent mind was the only possible explanation for the printing. How much more incredible is it to believe that the universe, in its infinite complexity, could have happened by chance?

The human body, for instance, is an admittedly astounding and complex organism, a continual marvel of organization, design and efficiency. So impressed was Albert Einstein with this that he concluded: "My religion consists of a humble admiration of the illuminate supe-

19

rior Spirit who reveals himself in the slight details we are able to perceive with our frail and feeble minds. That deeply emotional conviction of the presence of a superior reasoning power, which is revealed in the incomprehensible universe, forms my idea of God."[4] To our knowledge, he never progressed to believe in a personal God.

There are basically two choices for Christians and non-Christians alike: Did the universe and the human race begin by chance or by purpose and design?

Scientists have long relied on infinite time plus chance to explain the origin of life. This view for them avoids the *unacceptable conclusion* of divine cause. The process itself requires certain presuppositions and conditions or else no life would generate. For this to have happened there must have been

- an ideally prepared primordial soup
- frequent jolts of electrical charges
- unlimited period of time—eons and eons

Life forms then would evolve. However, the difficulties this theory presents are so enormous that today those same scientists are forthrightly pointing out its weaknesses.

The distinguished astronomer Sir Fred Hoyle has proposed an analogy to illustrate these difficulties. He asks, "How long would it take a blindfolded person to solve a Rubik's Cube?" If the person made one move per second, without resting, Hoyle estimates it would take an astonishing 1.35 trillion years! Therefore, he concludes, when you consider the life expectancy of a human being, a blindfolded person could not solve the Rubik's Cube.

Hoyle then explains that it would be equally as difficult for the accidental formation of only one of the many chains of amino acids in a living cell in which there are about 200,000 such amino acids. Now if you would compute the time required to get all 200,000 amino acids for one human cell to come together by chance, it would be about 293.5 times the estimated age of the earth (set at the standard 4.6 billion years). The odds against this happening would be far greater than a blindfolded person trying to solve the Rubik's Cube!

Hoyle offers another analogy, characterizing it as the "junkyard mentality": "What are the chances that a tornado might blow through a junkyard containing all the parts of a 747, accidentally assemble them into a plane, and leave it ready for takeoff?" Hoyle answers, "The possibilities are so small as to be negligible even if a tornado were to blow through enough junkyards to fill the whole universe!"

In his impressive book *The Intelligent Universe,* Hoyle concludes, "As biochemists discover more and more about the awesome complexity of life, it is apparent that its chances of originating by accident are so minute that they can be completely ruled out. Life cannot have arisen by chance."[5]

ORDER AND DESIGN IN THE UNIVERSE

When we speak of design as opposed to chance, we are referring to the observable parts of our world, the smallest of neutrons and protons, and the vastness of the galaxies. Who or what gave the original specifications and information that put it all together? This information is what we mean by design. It would be comparable to looking for the master plan that took glass, metal and phosphorous and formed these materials into a functioning TV. No one would think of suggesting that "natural selection" or self-assembly produced such a product. Indeed, the term "natural selection" would not be an explanation, it would only be a label. It would not tell us how these parts knew enough to form together for a useful end. Someone had the information that programmed those parts into a TV.

In the same way, the physical systems of our universe loudly proclaim that someone programmed the instructions into the individual parts to produce the world we see. Dr. Robert Gange suggests it would be valid to say that it was *intentionally* designed. If someone should claim that living structures can be traced to the physical properties of subnuclear particles, there are questions that call for an answer:

• How did these particles arise?

• Why does an electron have exactly the electrical charge and mass that it does?

• Who or what dialed the value of the gravitational "constant"?

• Why is it that light travels at precisely the speed it does?[6]

From the myriad examples we could cite of intentional design, consider the remarkable properties of plain water. Dr. L. J. Henderson enumerates some of these properties that imply intentionality.

> *Water has a high specific heat.* Therefore, the chemical reactions within the [human] body are kept rather stable. If water had a *low* specific heat we would "boil over" with the least activity. If we raise the temperature of a solution by ten degrees Centigrade we speed up the reaction by two. *Without this particular property of water, life would hardly be possible.*

21

The ocean is the world's thermostat, as we have learned from El Niño. It takes a large loss of heat for water to pass from liquid to ice, and for water to become steam quite an intake of energy is required. Hence the ocean is a cushion against the heat of the sun and the freezing blast of the winter. Unless the temperatures of the earth's surface were modulated by the ocean and kept within certain limits, life would either be cooked to death or frozen to death.

Water is the universal solvent. It dissolves acids, bases and salts. Chemically it is relatively inert providing a medium for reactions without [being involved] in them. In the human blood stream water holds in solution the minimum of *sixty-four substances.* . . . Any other solvent would be a pure sludge. Without the particular property of water, life as we know it would be impossible.[7]

The earth itself is evidence of meticulous design. "If it were much smaller, our atmosphere would be impossible (as on Mercury and the moon); if much larger the atmosphere would contain free hydrogen (as on Jupiter and Saturn). Its distance from the sun is very precise—even a small change would make it too hot or too cold. Our moon, probably responsible for the continents and ocean basins, is unique in our solar system and seems to have originated in a way quite different from the other relatively smaller moons. The tilt of the earth's axis insures the seasons."[8]

Equally amazing examples of design can be seen within living things, including humans. There are a*pproximately eleven million species of life on earth,* and each one is a living miracle. They are the result of mind-boggling organizational intricacies at the molecular level that leave us in awe. Consider the human eye. The English theologian William Paley pointed to the "fitting together efficiently and cooperatively of the lens, retina and brain; enabling humans to have vision; as conclusive evidence of the design of an all-wise Creator. Thus the functional design of organisms and their features are taken as evidence of the existence of the Designer."[9]

Even Darwin himself in a chapter from his *The Origins of Species* titled "Difficulties with the Theory" states: "To suppose that the eye, with so many parts all working together . . . could have formed by natural selection, seems, I freely confess, absurd in the highest degree." Harvard's Richard Lewontin, an evolutionist, states that organisms "appear to have been carefully and artfully designed" and calls the perfection of organisms "the chief evidence of a Supreme Designer."[10]

THE UNIVERSE HAD A BEGINNING

In addition to design in the universe, there is the implication that the universe had in some sense a beginning—a moment in time that brought the world into being. The Bible describes it this way: "In the beginning you [LORD] laid the foundations of the earth, and the heavens are the work of your hands" (Psalm 102:25).

Scientists avoided the idea that time had a beginning or an end since it suggested divine intervention. Through the years a number of alternative theories were developed.

• One attempt was the *"continuous creation/steady-state"* model of the universe proposed in 1948 by Hermann Bondi, Fred Hoyle and Tom Gold. This model was described by Dr. James Brooks: "In the steady-state model, it was proposed that as the galaxies moved farther away from each other, new galaxies were formed in between, out of matter that was being 'continually created.' The universe would therefore look more or less the same at all times and its density would be roughly constant. This projected model suggests matter (in the form of hydrogen) is always being created from nothing, and comes about in order to counteract the dilution of material which occurs as the galaxies drift away from each other."[11] His conclusion from this and other factors is that the universe had no beginning and is eternal.

Dr. Robert Jastrow, founder of NASA's Institute for Space Studies, explains that the opposite is true. The moment a star is born, it begins to *consume* some of the hydrogen in the universe, and there is a continual dilution of both hydrogen and the heavier metals in the universe today. He concludes that the theory of an eternal universe is untenable.[12]

• A second explanation posed by scientists for the beginning of the universe has been called the *"oscillating model."* This says that the universe is like a spring, expanding and contracting, repeating the cycle indefinitely. The basis of this theory is that the universe is "closed," that is, no new energy is being put into it. The expansion of matter would reach a certain point and the force of gravity would pull everything together before expanding again. However, all the evidence refutes this position; the universe is clearly losing density with no sign that the persistent expansion ever has or ever will reverse, and thus is not closed.

Dr. William L. Craig gives his conclusions about these two models

23

with: "Both the steady state and oscillating models of the universe fail to fit the facts of observational cosmology. Therefore we can conclude once more that the universe began to exist."[13]

• A third view of the beginning of the universe became known as the *"big bang"* theory. Dr. Edwin Hubble plotted the speeds of the galaxies and confirmed that all the galaxies are moving apart from us and one another at enormous speeds. The law bearing his name states: The farther away a galaxy is, the faster it moves.

The staggering implication of this is that at one time all matter was packed into a dense mass at temperatures of many trillions of degrees. Scientists who observed this phenomenon theorized the universe must have originally resembled a white-hot fireball in the very first moments after the big bang occurred.

A confirmation of this theory came in 1965 when two physicists made the surprising discovery the earth was entirely bathed in *a faint glow of radiation*. Its waves followed the exact pattern of wavelength expected in a giant explosion. Scientists, since then, have reconfirmed there could be no other obvious explanation than that these radiation waves were the aftermath of the big bang.

BEFORE THE BIG BANG

Dr. Robert Jastrow, who states that he is an agnostic in religious matters, comments on the theory of the big bang:

> Now we see how the astronomical evidence leads to a biblical view of the origin of the world. The details differ, but the essential elements in the astronomical and biblical accounts of Genesis are the same. The chain of events leading to man commenced suddenly and sharply at a definite moment in time, in a flash of light and energy.
>
> Scientists have traditionally rejected the thought of a natural phenomenon which cannot be explained, even with unlimited time and money. There is a kind of religion in science; every event can be explained in a rational way as the product of some previous event; every effect must have its cause. Now science has proven that the universe exploded into existence at a specific moment. It asks, "What cause produced this effect? Who or what put the matter and energy into the universe?" And science does not answer these questions.

Jastrow concludes with this monumental statement:

> For the scientist who has lived by his faith in the *power of reason,* the story ends like a bad dream. He has scaled the mountains of ignorance; he is about to conquer the highest peak; as he pulls himself over the final rock, he is greeted by a band of theologians who have been sitting there for centuries.[14]

For many, this is an exceedingly strange development, unexpected by all but the theologians. They have always accepted the word of the Bible. In the beginning God created heaven and earth.

One of those theologians, David, said knowingly, "The heavens declare the glory of God; the skies proclaim the work of his hands" (Psalm 19:1). And the apostle Paul wrote, "God has made it plain. . . . For since the creation of the world God's invisible qualities—his eternal power and divine nature—have been clearly seen, being understood from what has been made, so that men are without excuse" (Romans 1:19-20). To which Augustine added, "Who can understand this mystery or explain it to others?"

THE MORAL ARGUMENT

Yet another evidence for the existence of God is what C. S. Lewis calls "right and wrong as a clue to the meaning of the universe." There is an influence or a command inside each of us trying to get us to behave in a certain way. Lewis explains that universally we find people commonly appeal to some sense of right and wrong. People argue with one another "That's my seat. I had it first! Suppose I did the same to you! How would you like it? Come on, you promised." Educated as well as uneducated people say things like this every day, children as well as grown-ups.

In these arguments there is an appeal to some behavioral standard that the other person is assumed to accept. The person had a good reason to do it; it was okay to do it.

The appeal is to some *law or rule of fair play or morality* that's built in them both. Rarely does the other person say, "Who cares about your standard?" It is there between them. They don't question it. As Lewis puts it, "Quarreling means trying to show the other man is in the wrong."

This law has to do with what ought to take place. Somehow we know it inside of us. It is not just a set of cultural norms or cultural standards. Also, there is a surprising consensus from civilization to civilization about what is moral decency. And we all do agree some moralities are better than others. "If no set of moral ideas were truer or better than any other, there would be no sense in preferring civilized morality to savage morality, or Christian morality to Nazi morality."[15]

Lewis says the moral law cannot be merely a social convention. It is more like a mathematical table, he tells us. We would never say the math table is a social convention made up to help us and that we could have made differently if we wanted to. Two plus two will always equal four irrespective of its culture. Hence, if there is a moral law, there must be a moral Lawgiver. The Bible describes humankind as "made in God's own image," distinguishing the human person from all other creatures. This moral image comes with us at birth regardless of our origins or nationality. Our favorite pet never asks, "Is this right or wrong?" or "Is this good or bad?" Such ideas are unique to human beings, and for human beings the moral image is not optional software.

Our favorite pet never asks, "Is this right or wrong?" or "Is this good or bad?"

Yes, there is Somebody behind the universe. He is a God who has mind, emotions, conscience and will himself—a complete personality. These ingredients were given to us when he created us, and they include a moral law. He is intensely interested in right conduct—in fair play, unselfishness, courage, good faith, honesty and truthfulness.

> God's law is not something alien, imposed on us from without, but woven into the very fabric of our being at creation. There is something deep within us that echoes God's yes and no, right and wrong. (Romans 2:15 The Message)

GOD—A CELESTIAL KILLJOY?

It is important to observe here that though there are many indications of God in nature, we could never know conclusively from nature that he exists or what he is like. The question was asked centuries ago, "Can you fathom the mysteries of God?" (Job 11:7). The answer is no! Unless God reveals himself, we are doomed to confusion and conjecture.

It is obvious that among those who believe in God there are many ideas abroad today as to what God is like.

• Some, for instance, believe God to be a celestial killjoy. They view him as peering over the balcony of heaven looking for anyone who seems to be enjoying life. On finding such a person, he shouts down, "Cut it out."

• Others think of God as a sentimental grandfather of the sky, rocking benignly and stroking his beard as he says, "Boys will be boys." That everything will work out in the end, no matter what you have done, is conceded to be his general attitude toward people.

• Others think of him as a big ball of fire and of us as little sparks who will eventually gravitate back to the big ball. Still others, like Einstein, think of God as an impersonal force or mind.

• To the deist, God created the world and yet never intrudes on it. He wound up the clock, and now he is letting it run down.

• To the theist, however, God is the Creator and Ruler; he is personally involved with his creation while revealing himself.

Herbert Spencer, one of the popularizers of agnosticism of a century ago, observed accurately that a bird has never been known to fly out into space. Therefore, he concluded by analogy that it is impossible for the finite to penetrate the infinite. Even if God does exist we can never know him personally or anything about his existence.

Spencer was right when he observed that birds never fly out into space. His observation was correct, but his conclusion missed an important alternative possibility: God, the infinite Creator, could penetrate our finiteness—*the infinite could penetrate the finite,* thereby communicating to us what he is really like. This, of course, is what God did.

GOD HAS PENETRATED THE FINITE

As the writer to the Hebrews puts it: "In the past God spoke to our forefathers through the prophets at many times and in various ways, but in these last days he has spoken to us by his Son, whom he appointed heir of all things, and through whom he made the universe" (Hebrews 1:1-2).

God has indeed taken the initiative throughout history to communicate to man. His fullest revelation has been his invasion into human history in the person of Jesus Christ. Here, in terms of human personality, we can understand him because he has lived among us.

If you wanted to communicate your love to a colony of ants, how could you most effectively do it? Clearly, it would be best to become an ant. Only in this way could your existence and what you were like be communicated fully and effectively. In a very dim way this pictures what God did for us to make himself clearly known. We are, as J. B. Phillips aptly put it, "the visited planet." The best and clearest answer to how we know there is a God is that he has visited us. The other indications we've discussed are merely clues or hints. What confirms them conclusively is the birth, life, death and resurrection of Jesus Christ.

Invisible does not mean unreal.

CHANGED LIVES

Other evidence for the reality of God's existence is his clear presence in the lives of men and women today. Where Jesus Christ is believed and trusted, a profound change takes place in the individual, and ultimately, the community. One of the most moving illustrations of this is recorded by Ernest Gordon, a prisoner of war who later became chaplain at Princeton University. In his *Through the Valley of the Kwai* he tells how, during World War II, the prisoners of the Japanese on the Malay peninsula had been reduced almost to animals, stealing food from others who were also starving. In their desperation, the prisoners decided it would be good to read the New Testament.

Because Gordon was a university graduate, they asked him to lead. By his own admission he was a skeptic, and those who asked him to lead them were unbelievers too. He and others came to trust Jesus Christ on becoming acquainted with him in all of his beauty and power through the uncluttered simplicity of the New Testament. How this group of scrounging, clawing humans was transformed into a community of love is a touching and powerful story demonstrating clearly the reality of God in Jesus Christ. Many others today, in less dramatic terms, have experienced this same reality.

There is, then, convincing evidence from creation, history and contemporary life that there is a God, and this God can be known in personal experience.

FOR FURTHER READING

Lewis, C. S. *Mere Christianity*. New York: Macmillan, 1986.

Packer, J. I. *Knowing God*. Twentieth anniv. ed. Downers Grove, Ill.: InterVarsity Press, 1993.

Little, Paul E. *Know Who You Believe*. Colorado Springs: Victor Books, 2003.

CHAPTER THREE

IS CHRIST GOD?

It is impossible for us to know conclusively whether God exists and what he is like unless *he takes the initiative* and reveals himself. Without his initiative and self-revelation we are left to conjecture, unfounded opinion or prejudice. Legitimately we ask what he is like and what is his attitude toward us. If we were certain he existed but learned he was like Adolf Hitler—capricious, vicious, prejudiced and cruel, what a horrible realization that would be!

A brief scan of the horizon of history gives us some clue to God personally revealing himself. One clear clue stands out. In an obscure village in Palestine two thousand years ago a child, who was said to be "king of the Jews," was born in a stable. His birth was feared by the reigning monarch, Herod. In an attempt to destroy this baby, King Herod gave orders to kill all the boys two years old and under who were born in Bethlehem. In vain he hoped to destroy any rival. History has called this the "slaughter of the innocents" (Matthew 2:1-18).

His birth split time in two! This child's life was destined to change the course of history. Two thousand years ago, his coming rocked the world. It changed its calendar, tailored its mores. The atheist in America dates his checks with a year dating approximately from Jesus' birth. The rulers of countries, both East and West, regardless of their religions, use his approximate birth year. Unthinkingly, we declare his birth on letters, legal documents and date books. On the day we set aside to remember his birth, the mall parking lots are starkly empty.

This baby, whose birthday we still celebrate, and his parents settled in Nazareth, where he learned his earthly father's trade of carpentry. From the beginning he was an unusual child. When he was twelve years old, he confounded the scholars and rabbis in the Jerusalem synagogue with his questions. His parents remonstrated with him because he stayed behind after they departed, and he made the mystifying reply, "Didn't you know I had to be in my Father's [God's] house?" (Luke 2:49). His answer implied a unique relationship between God and himself.

This young man lived in obscurity until he was thirty, and then he began a public ministry lasting three years. He was known as a kindly person, and we are told "the common people heard him gladly." He stood out from other teachers of his day in that "he taught as one who had authority, and not as their teachers of the law" (Matthew 7:29).

JESUS SAID HE WAS THE SON OF GOD

It soon became apparent in many ways that Jesus was making shocking and startling statements about himself. He began to identify himself as far more than a remarkable teacher or a prophet. He began to say clearly that he was deity. He made his identity the focal point of his teaching. The all-important question he put to those who followed him was, "Who do you say I am?" Peter answered his question with, "You are the Christ, the Son of the living God" (Matthew 16:15-16). Jesus was not shocked, nor did he rebuke Peter. On the contrary, he commended him.

Jesus made the claim to be the Son of God explicitly. His hearers got the full impact of his words. We are told, "The Jews tried all the harder to kill him; not only was he breaking the Sabbath, but he was even calling God his own Father, making himself equal with God" (John 5:18).

Christianity is not a *path* but a *person,* not *rules* but a *relationship.*

On another occasion he said, "I and the Father are one" (John 10:30). Immediately the Jews wanted to stone him. He asked them for which good work they wanted to kill him. They replied, "We are not stoning you for any of these, . . . but for blasphemy, because you, a mere man, claim to be God" (John 10:33).

Jesus claimed and demonstrated the attributes that only God has. When a paralytic was let down through a roof and placed at his feet, he said, "Son, your sins are forgiven" (Mark 2:5). This caused a great ruckus among the scribes, who said in their hearts, "Why does this fellow talk like that? He's blaspheming! Who can forgive sins but God alone?" (Mark 2:7).

Jesus, knowing their thoughts, said to them, "Which is easier: to say to the paralytic, 'Your sins are forgiven,' or to say, 'Get up, take your mat and walk'?" (Mark 2:8-9). In effect he answered their question with: "That you may know that I, the Son of Man, have authority on earth to forgive sins [which you rightly say God alone can do], but since this cannot be seen, I'll do something you can see" (Mark 2:10). Turning to the palsied man, he commanded him, "I tell you, get up, take your mat and go home" (Mark 2:11). The man got up and walked!

The title *Son of Man* is one Jesus used to refer to himself, but always with some assertion of deity. In his words concerning his coming Jesus speaks of himself as the Son of Man come "to give his life a ransom for many." This is not a disclaimer of deity, by any means. Rather the title embraces both his deity and his coming as a part of the human race. His authority, miracles, teaching and character were traits true only of God.

At the critical moment when his life was at stake because of these claims, the high priest put the question to him directly:

> "Are you the Christ, the Son of the Blessed One?"
> "I am," said Jesus calmly, "and you will see the Son of Man sitting at the right hand of the Mighty One [God] and coming on the clouds of heaven." The high priest tore his clothes and asked, "Why do we need any more witnesses? You have heard the blasphemy." (Mark 14:61-64)

John Stott sums it up.

> So close was his identification with God that it was natural for him to equate a man's attitude to himself with his attitude to God. Thus,
> to know him was to know God;
> to see him was to see God;
> to believe in him was to believe in God;
> to receive him was to receive God;
> to hate him was to hate God;
> to honour him was to honour God.[1]

Only Four Possibilities

As we face the claims of Christ to deity, there are only four possibilities. He was either a liar, a lunatic, a legend or the Truth. If we say he is not the Truth, our reasoning takes us automatically to affirming one of the other three alternatives, whether we realize it or not. It is helpful to examine these possibilities.

1. *Did Jesus lie by saying he was God when he knew he was not God?* If so, he deliberately deceived his hearers to lend authority to himself and his teaching. Few if any seriously hold this position. Even those who deny his deity affirm Jesus as a *great moral teacher.* They fail to realize those two views are a contradictory. Jesus could hardly be a great moral teacher if, on the most crucial point of his teaching—his identity—he was a deliberate liar.

2. *Was he a lunatic?* To take this position would take considerable contortion of the evidence. In fact, there is no evidence to support this view. Rather, all the evidence points in the other direction. It may seem kinder, though no less shocking, to say he was sincere but self-deceived. A person today who thinks he is God or a fried taco might be unkindly designated as "lunatic," and we would offer help. However, the term would be ludicrous if applied to Jesus Christ.

As we look at the life of Christ, we see no evidence of the abnormality and imbalance common in a deranged person. Rather, we find the greatest composure under pressure. At his trial before Pilate, when his very life was at stake, he was calm and serene. As C. S. Lewis put it, "The discrepancy between the depth and sanity of His moral teaching and a diagnosis of rampant megalomania" are patently incompatible.[2]

3. *Was he a legend?* This third alternative of Jesus' claims and supernatural power are all the invention of his enthusiastic followers, therefore are a legend. It has even been rumored that his claim to be God, the teachings he gave and his miracles were added to until the third and fourth centuries. Words were put into his mouth that he would have been shocked to hear. Were he to return he would immediately repudiate them.

However, modern archaeological discoveries have fundamentally refuted the legend theory. In particular, three statements are especially conclusive:

• It has been conclusively proven that the four biographies of Christ (Matthew, Mark, Luke and John) were written within the lifetime of contemporaries of Christ.

• "There is no reason to believe any of the Gospels were written later than A.D. 70," concluded world-famous archaeologist Dr. William F. Albright.

• For a mere legend about Christ, in the form of the gospel, to have gained the circulation and to have had the impact it had, without one shred of basis in fact, is incredible.

Jesus Christ's being a legend would require as fantastic a scenario as someone in our own time writing a biography of the late John F. Kennedy in which it is asserted that Kennedy claimed to be God, to forgive people's sins, and to have risen from the dead. Such a story is so wild it would never get off the ground because there are still too many people around who knew the man! The legend theory does not hold water in the light of the logic and early date of the Gospel manuscripts.

4. *Jesus spoke the truth—He was God come to earth.* From one point of view, claims don't mean much. Talk is cheap. Anyone can make claims, and many could be named from around the world. I could claim to be God, and you could claim to be God, but the question all of us must answer is, "What credentials do we bring to substantiate our claim?" In my case it wouldn't take five minutes to disprove my claim. It probably wouldn't take too much more to dispose of yours.

But when it comes to Jesus of Nazareth, it's not so simple. He had the credentials to back up his claim. He said, "Even though you do not believe me, believe the miracles, that you may know and understand that the Father is in me, and I in the Father" (John 10:38).

WHAT WERE JESUS' CREDENTIALS?

Jesus' moral character coincided with his claims. We saw earlier that many asylum inmates claim to be celebrities or deities but their claims are belied by their characters. Not so with Christ. And we do not compare Christ with others; we contrast all others with him. He is unique—as unique as God.

1. Jesus Christ was sinless. The caliber of his life was such that he was able to challenge his enemies with the question, "Can any of you prove me guilty of sin?" (John 8:46). He was met by silence, even though he addressed those who would have liked to point out a flaw in his character.

We read of the temptations of Jesus, but we never hear of a confession of sin on his part. He never asked for forgiveness, though he told his followers to do so. This lack of any sense of moral failure on Jesus' part is completely contrary to the accounts of the saints and mystics in all ages. The closer men and women draw to God, the more overwhelmed they are with their own failure, corruption and short-coming. This is true also, in the moral realm, for ordinary mortals. The closer one is to a shining light, the more he or she realizes the need for a bath.

His followers like John, Paul and Peter, all of whom were trained from earliest childhood to believe in the univer-sality of sin, all spoke of the sinlessness of Jesus: "He committed no sin, and no deceit was found in his mouth" (1 Peter 2:22); "In him is no sin" (1 John 3:5); Jesus "had no sin" (2 Corinthians 5:21). Pilate, no friend of Jesus, said, "I find no basis for a charge against him" (John 18:38). He implicitly recognized Christ's innocence. And the Roman centurion who witnessed the death of Christ said "Surely he was the Son of God!" (Matthew 27:54).

2. In Jesus Christ we find the perfect personality. Bernard Ramm points out:

34

Jesus said he was the only way to God. One way is not narrow if it's the *true* way.

• The airline pilot can land on only *one* runway.

• In the United States there is only *one* right side of the road to drive on.

> If God were a man, we would expect His personality to be true humanity. Only God could tell us what a true man should be like. Certainly there are forerunners of piety in Old Testament models. Foremost must be a complete consciousness, coupled with a complete dedication and consecration of life to God. Then, ranked below this, are the other virtues, graces and attributes that characterize perfect humanity. Intelligence must not stifle piety, and prayer must not be a substitute for work, and zeal must not be irrational fanaticism, and reserve must not become stolidity.

In Christ we have the perfect blend of personality traits, because as God incarnate, he is perfect humanity. John Schaff describes:

> Jesus' zeal never degenerated into passion, nor his constancy into obstinacy, nor his benevolence into

weakness, nor his tenderness into sentimentality. His unworldliness was free from indifference and unsociability or undue familiarity; His self-denial from moroseness; His temperance from austerity. He combined childlike innocence with manly strength, absorbing devotion to God with untiring interest in the welfare of man, tender love to the sinner with uncompromising severity against sin, commanding dignity with winning humility, fearless courage with wise caution, unyielding firmness with sweet gentleness!"[3]

3. Christ demonstrated a power over natural forces that could belong only to God, the Author of these forces. He stilled a raging storm of wind and waves on the Sea of Galilee. In doing this he provoked from those in the boat the awestruck question, "Who is this? Even the wind and the waves obey him" (Mark 4:41). He turned water into wine and fed five thousand people from five loaves and two fish, gave a grieving widow back her only son by raising him from the dead and brought to life the dead daughter of a shattered father. To a friend he said, "Lazarus, come forth!" and dramatically raised him from the dead.

It is most significant that his enemies did not deny this miracle. Rather, they tried to kill him. "If we let him go on like this," they said, "everyone will believe in him" (John 11:48).

4. Jesus demonstrated the Creator's power over sickness and disease. He made the lame to walk, the dumb to speak and the blind to see. Some of his healings were congenital problems not susceptible to psychosomatic cure. The most outstanding was that of the blind man whose case is recorded in John 9. Though the man couldn't answer his speculative questioners, his experience was enough to convince him. "One thing I do know. I was blind but now I see," he declared (John 9:25). He was astounded that his friends didn't recognize his healer as the Son of God. "Nobody has ever heard of opening the eyes of a man born blind," he said (John 9:32). To him the evidence was obvious.

5. Jesus' supreme credential to authenticate his claim to deity was his resurrection from the dead. Five times in the course of his life he predicted he would die. He also predicted how he would die and that three days later he would rise from the dead and appear to his disciples (Matthew 16:21; 17:22-23; Mark 8:31; 10:32-33; Luke 9:22). Surely this was the great test. It was a claim that was easy to verify. It

either happened or it didn't.

The resurrection is so crucial and foundational a subject I will devote a whole chapter to it. If the resurrection happened, there is no difficulty with any other miracles. And if we establish the resurrection, we have the answer to the big question of God, his character and our relationship to him. An answer to this question makes it possible to answer all subsidiary questions.

Christ moved history as only God could do. Schaff rounds out his picture of the Jesus portrayed in the New Testament:

> This Jesus of Nazareth without money and arms, conquered more millions than Alexander, Caesar, Muhammad and Napoleon; without science and learning, he shed more light on matters human and divine than all philosophers and scholars combined; without the eloquence of schools, he spoke such words of life as were never spoken before or since and produced effects which lie beyond the reach of orator or poet; without writing a single line, he set more pens in motion and furnished themes for more sermons, orations, discussions, learned volumes, works of art and songs of praise than the whole army of great men of ancient and modern times.[4]

6. Finally, we know that Christ is God because we can experience him in the twentieth century. Experience in itself is not conclusive, but combined with the historic objective truth of the resurrection it gives us the basis for our solid conviction. There is no other hypothesis to explain all the data we have than the profound fact that Jesus Christ is God the Son.

The greatest favor we can do for people, therefore, is to introduce them to this Jesus Christ.

FOR FURTHER READING

Bruce, F. F. *Jesus: Lord and Savior.* Downers Grove, Ill.: InterVarsity Press; London: Hodder & Stoughton, 1986.

Kreeft, Peter. *Between Heaven and Hell.* Downers Grove, Ill.: InterVarsity Press, 1982.

CHAPTER FOUR

DID CHRIST RISE FROM THE DEAD?

Both friends and enemies of Christianity have recognized the resurrection of Jesus Christ to be the foundation stone of the faith. In the early church at Corinth some were questioning, even denying, the possibility of the resurrection of the dead. Hearing this, the apostle Paul gave the astute summary statement "If Christ has not been raised, our preaching is useless and so is your faith" (1 Corinthians 15:14). With these few words Paul soundly rested his whole case on the bodily resurrection of Jesus Christ. Either Jesus did or did not rise from the dead. If he did, it was the most sensational event in all of history and gives us conclusive answers to the most profound questions of our existence:

- Where have we come from?
- Why are we here?
- What is our future destiny?

If Christ rose, we know with certainty that God exists, what he is like and that he cares for each of us individually. The universe, then, takes on meaning and purpose, and we can experience the living God in contemporary life. These and many other life-expanding things are true if Jesus of Nazareth rose from the dead.

NOT WISHFUL THINKING

On the other hand, if Christ did not rise from the dead, Christianity is an interesting museum piece and nothing more. It has no objective validity or reality. Though it is a nice, wishful thought, it certainly isn't worth getting steamed up about. The martyrs in early centuries went unwaveringly into the den of lions, singing as they went! In this century nationals and missionaries on other continents have given their lives uselessly and have been poor deluded fools.

Attacks on Christianity by dissenters have most often concentrated on the resurrection. It has been correctly seen as the keystone to the entire Christian faith. A remarkable plan of assault was contemplated in the early 1930s by a young British lawyer. He was convinced the resurrection was a mere tissue of fable and fantasy. Sensing it was the foundation of the faith, he decided to do the world a favor by once and for all exposing this fraud and superstition. As a lawyer, he felt he had the critical faculties to rigidly sift evidence and to admit nothing as evidence that did not meet the stiff criteria for admission into a law court today.

> **We can connect with him. He is** *alive!*

However, while Frank Morison was doing his research, a remarkable thing happened. The case was not nearly as easy as he had supposed. As a result the first chapter in his book *Who Moved the Stone?* is entitled "The Book That Refused to Be Written." In it he described how, as he examined the evidence, he became persuaded against his will of the fact of the bodily resurrection.

DATA TO BE CONSIDERED

What are some of the pieces of data to be considered in answering the question, "Did Christ rise from the dead?"

• *First, there is the fact of the Christian church.* It is worldwide in scope. Its history can be traced back to Palestine around A.D. 32. The book of Acts is a litany of stories relating how whole communities were stirred by the message of Jesus and his resurrection. The believers were first called Christians in the city of Antioch. In Thessalonica Paul's preaching persuaded some of the Jews, a large number of God-fearing Greeks and not a few prominent women to believe. The message literally "turned the world of their time upside down" (Acts 17:6 KJV). They constantly referred to the resurrection as the basis for their teaching, preaching, living and—significantly—dying.

• *Then there is the fact of the Christian day. Sunday is the day of worship for Christians.* Its history can also be traced back to the year A.D. 32. Such a shift in the calendar was monumental. Something cataclysmic must have happened to change the day of worship from the Jewish sabbath, the seventh day of the week, to Sunday, the first day. Acts 20:7 states simply, "On the first day of the week we came together," an established pattern. Christians said the shift came because of their desire to celebrate the day Jesus rose from the dead. This shift is all the more remarkable when we remember that the first Christians were Jews. If the resurrection does not account for this change, what does?

• *There is the Christian book, the New Testament.* In its pages are contained independent testimonies to the fact of the resurrection. Three of these, at least, are eyewitnesses: John, Peter and Matthew.

Luke's Gospel gives evidence of a historian with a classical background known to travel with Paul and heard him preach the resurrection (2 Timothy 4:11). Paul, writing to the churches at an early date, referred to the resurrection in such a way that to him and his readers the event was obviously well-known and accepted without question. Are these men who helped transform the moral structure of society consummate liars or deluded madmen? These alternatives stem from our human knowledge and are harder to believe than the fact of Jesus, the incarnation of God rising from the dead. There is no shred of evidence to support another view.

For intelligent belief, two facets of the resurrection require explanation by believer and unbeliever alike. They are the empty tomb and the alleged appearances of Jesus Christ following his burial.

39

ACCOUNTING FOR THE EMPTY TOMB

• *The earliest explanation circulated was that the disciples stole the body!* In Matthew 28:11-15, we have the record of the reaction of the chief priests and the elders when the guards gave them the infuriating and mysterious news that the body was gone. These religious leaders gave the soldiers money and told them to say the disciples had come at night and stolen the body while they were asleep. This story was so obviously false Matthew didn't even bother to refute it! What judge would listen to you if you said your neighbor came into your house and stole your television set while you were asleep? Who knows what goes on while he's asleep? Testimony like this would be laughed out of any court.

Furthermore, we are faced with a psychological and ethical impossibility. Stealing the body of Christ is something totally foreign to the character of the disciples and all we know of them. It would mean they were perpetrators of a deliberate lie resulting in the deception and ultimate death of thousands of people. It is inconceivable that even a few of the disciples could have conspired together and pulled off a theft of the body and never tell the others.

Every one of the disciples faced the test of torture, and all but the apostle John were martyred for their teachings and beliefs. People will die for what they believe to be true, though it may actually be false. They do not, however, die for what they know is a lie. If ever a person tells the truth, it is on his or her deathbed. And if the disciples had taken the body and Christ were still dead, how would we explain the problem of his alleged appearances?

• *A second hypothesis is that the authorities, Jewish or Roman, moved the body.* But why? Having put special Roman guards at the tomb, what would the Romans gain by moving the body? The convincing answer for this thesis is the silence of these authorities in the face of the apostles' bold preaching in Jerusalem about the resurrection. The ecclesiastical leaders were seething with rage and did everything possible to prevent the spread of this message and to suppress it (Acts 4). They arrested Peter and John, and beat and threatened them in an attempt to close their mouths.

For either the Jewish or Roman authorities, there was a very simple solution to their problem. If either of them had Christ's body, they could have paraded it through the streets of Jerusalem. In one fell swoop they would have successfully smothered Christianity in its cradle. That they did not do this bears eloquent testimony to the fact that they did not have the body.

• *Another popular theory, called the wrong tomb theory, suggests the distraught women, overcome with grief, missed their way in the dimness of the morning.* In their distress they imagined Christ had risen because the tomb was empty.

This theory, however, falls before the same fact that destroys the previous one. If the women went to the wrong tomb, why did the high priests and other enemies of the faith not go to the right tomb and produce the body? Further, it is inconceivable that all of Jesus' followers would succumb to the same mistake. Certainly Joseph of Arimathea, owner of the tomb, would have solved the problem. In addition, it must be remembered that this was a private burial ground, not a public cemetery, as we envision it. There was no other tomb nearby that would have allowed them to make this mistake.

• *The swoon theory has also been advanced to explain the empty tomb.* In this view, Christ did not actually die. He was mistakenly reported to be dead but had swooned from exhaustion, pain and loss of blood. When he was laid in the coolness of the tomb, he revived. He came out of the tomb and appeared to his disciples, and they mistakenly thought he had risen from the dead.

This is a theory of modern construction. It first appeared at the end of the eighteenth century. It is significant that no suggestion of this kind has come down from antiquity among all the violent attacks that have been made on Christianity. All of the earliest records are emphatic about Jesus' death and shedding of blood.

For a moment, let us assume Christ was buried alive and swooned. Is it possible to believe he would have survived three days in a damp tomb without food or water or attention of any kind? Would he have survived being wound in seventy-five pounds of spice-laden graveclothes? Would he have had the strength to extricate himself from the graveclothes, push the heavy stone away from the mouth of the grave, overcome the Roman guards and walk miles on feet that had been pierced with spikes? Then, at that point, would he have the strength to present himself as a glorious and majestic God to be worshiped? Such a belief is more fantastic than the simple fact of the resurrection itself.

Even the German critic David Strauss, who by no means believed in the resurrection, rejected this idea as incredible. He said:

> It is impossible that One who had just come forth from the grave half dead, who crept about weak and ill, who stood in the need of medical treatment, of bandaging, strengthening, and tender care, and who at last succumbed to suffering, could ever have given the disciples the impression that he was a conqueror over death and the grave; that he was the Prince of Life. This lay at the bottom of their future ministry. Such a resus-

Jesus Christ's life, death and resurrection assure us:

• **His purpose is to "rescue us" from sin.**

• **His power will give us "eternal life."**

• **His suffering demonstrates the extent of his love for us.**

41

citation could only have weakened the impression which He had made upon them in life and in death— or at the most, could have given in an elegiac voice— but could by no possibility have changed their sorrow into enthusiasm or elevated their reverence into worship.[1]

Finally, if this theory is correct, Christ himself was involved in flagrant lies. His disciples believed and preached that he was dead but came alive again. Jesus did nothing to dispel this belief, but rather encouraged it. The only theory that adequately explains the empty tomb is the resurrection of Jesus Christ from the dead. With other religionists, their tombs become shrines of worship. With Christ, however, the empty tomb is a place where Christians rejoice.

THE APPEARANCES OF CHRIST

The second piece of data that both believer and unbeliever must explain is the recorded appearances of Christ. Ten distinct appearances are recorded. These occurred from the morning of his resurrection to his ascension forty days later. They show great variety as to time, place and people. Two were to individuals, Peter and James. Other appearances were to the disciples as a group, and one was to five hundred assembled believers. Each one was at a different place. Some were in the garden near his tomb; some were in the Upper Room. One was on the road from Jerusalem to Emmaus, and some were far away in Galilee. Each appearance was characterized by different acts and words by Jesus.

Lies or legends cannot explain the empty tomb, nor can we dismiss the appearances of Christ on this kind of basis. The accounts are testimonies given by eyewitnesses—people who were there, had seen and interacted with him and were profoundly certain of the truth of their statements.

Logically one might propose hallucinations to discount these eyewitness accounts of Christ's appearances after crucifixion. At first this sounds like a plausible explanation of an otherwise supernatural event. It is plausible until we remember the common laws observed by modern medicine that apply to such psychological phenomena. As we relate these principles to the evidence at hand, we can see what at first seemed most plausible is, in fact, impossible.

Hallucinations occur generally in people who tend to be vividly imaginative and of a nervous makeup. But the appearances of Christ were to all sorts of people. True, some were sensitive, but there were also hardheaded fishermen like Peter and others of various dispositions.

Hallucinations are known to be extremely subjective and individual. For this reason, no two people have the same experience. In the case of the resurrection, Christ appeared not just to individuals but to groups, including one with more than five hundred people. Paul said more than half of these people were still alive and could tell about these events (1 Corinthians 15).

Hallucinations usually occur only at particular times and places, and they are associated with the events fancied. However, these appearances occurred both indoors and outdoors, in the morning, afternoon and evening.

In general, these psychic experiences occur over a long period of time and with some regularity. These appearances happened during a period of forty days and then stopped abruptly. No one ever said they happened again.

Perhaps the most conclusive indication of the fallacy of the hallucination theory is a fact often overlooked. In order to have an experience like this, one must so intensely want to believe that he or she projects something that isn't really there and attaches reality to this imagination. For instance, a mother who has lost a son in the war remembers how he used to come home from work every evening at 5:30. She sits in her rocking chair every afternoon, musing and meditating. Finally, she thinks she sees him come through the door and has a conversation with him. At this point she has lost contact with reality.

> **This is how God showed his love among us: he sent his one and only Son into the world that we might live through him.**
>
> *(1 John 4:9)*

43

PERSUADED AGAINST THEIR WILLS

One might think hallucination is what happened to the disciples regarding the resurrection. The fact is, the opposite took place— they were persuaded against their wills that Jesus had risen from the dead!

• Mary came to the tomb on the first Easter Sunday morning with spices in her hands. Why? To anoint the dead body of the Lord she loved. She was obviously not expecting to find him risen from the dead. In fact, when she first saw Jesus she mistook him for the gardener! It was only after he spoke to her and spoke her name that she realized who he was.

• When the other disciples heard, they didn't believe. The story seemed to them "as an idle tale."

• When the resurrected Jesus finally appeared to the disciples, they were frightened and thought they were seeing a ghost! They thought they were having a hallucination, and it jolted them. To convince them he finally said, "Touch me and see; a ghost does not have flesh and bones, as you see I have." He asked them if they had any food, and they gave him a piece of broiled fish. Luke didn't add the obvious—ghosts don't eat fish (Luke 24:36-43)!

• Finally, there is the classic case that remains in our language today—Thomas the doubter. He was not present when Jesus appeared to the disciples the first time. They told him about it, but he scoffed and would not believe. In effect, he said, "I'm from Missouri. I won't believe unless I'm shown. I'm an empiricist. Unless I can put my finger into the nail wounds in his hands and my hand into his side, I will not believe." He wasn't about to have a hallucination!

John gives us the graphic story (John 20) of Jesus' appearance to the disciples eight days later. He graciously invited Thomas to examine the evidence of his hands and his side. Thomas looked at him and fell down in worship: "My Lord and my God" (John 20:28).

To hold the hallucination theory in explaining the appearances of Christ, one must completely ignore the evidence.

What was it that changed a band of frightened, cowardly disciples into men of courage and conviction? What was it that changed Peter who, the night before the crucifixion, was so afraid for his own skin that three times he denied publicly that he even knew Jesus. Some fifty days later he became a roaring lion, risking his life by saying he had seen Jesus risen from the dead. It must be remembered that Peter preached his electric Pentecost sermon in Jerusalem, where all these events took place and his life was in danger. He was not in Galilee, miles away where no one could verify the facts and where his ringing statements might go unchallenged.

Only the bodily resurrection of Christ could have produced this change.

People Who Saw Jesus Alive	Bible References
Two women outside of Jerusalem	Matthew 28:9-10
Mary Magdalene	John 20:15-18
Two travelers on the road to Emmaus	Luke 24:13-32
Peter in Jerusalem	Luke 24:34
Ten disciples in the upper room	John 20:19-25
Eleven disciples in the upper room	John 20:26-31
Seven disciples fishing	John 21:1-23
Eleven disciples on the mountain in Galilee	Matthew 28:16-20
More than five hundred people	1 Corinthians 15:5
James	1 Corinthians 15:7
Disciples who watched Jesus ascending into heaven	Luke 24:44-49; Acts 1:3-8

Table 4.1. Resurrection appearances

CONTEMPORARY PROOF

Finally, there is evidence for the resurrection that is contemporary and personal. If Jesus Christ rose from the dead, he is alive today, ready to invade and change those who invite him into their lives. Thousands now living bear uniform testimony their lives have been revolutionized by Jesus Christ. He has transformed them as he promised he would. The proof of the pudding is in the eating.

The invitation still stands: "Taste and see that the LORD is good!" (Psalm 34:8). The avenue to accept the offer to connect with the living Christ is open to all.

In summary, then, we can agree with Canon B. F. Westcott, a brilliant scholar at Cambridge, who said, "Indeed, taking all the evidence together, it is not too much to say there is no historic incident better or more variously supported than the resurrection of Christ. Nothing but the antecedent assumption that it must be false could have suggested the idea of deficiency in the proof of it."[2]

FOR FURTHER READING

Green, Michael. *The Empty Cross of Christ.* Downers Grove, Ill.: InterVarsity Press, 1984.

Morison, Frank. *Who Moved the Stone?* Grand Rapids, Mich.: Zondervan, 1987.

Wegner, Paul D. *God Crucified: Monotheism and Christianity in the New Testament.* Grand Rapids, Mich.: Eerdmans, 1999.

CHAPTER FIVE

IS THE BIBLE GOD'S WORD?

I heard about a Christian family that prayed out loud together several times each day. One day the youngest son looked up at a picture of Jesus on the kitchen wall, stared at it and said thoughtfully, "Jesus, Jesus, Jesus. That's all I hear. But he don't say nothin' back!"

Fortunately for us, Jesus does say something back—in the Bible. The apostle Peter tells us God has communicated "everything we need for life and godliness through our knowledge of him [Jesus Christ]" (2 Peter 1:3). When we contemplate the Bible as containing all God wants us to know for godliness, our perspective can change. This is not an insignificant book. "Read the instructions," our Designer reminds us.

Still it is valid to ask, is the Bible God's word? How do we know the Bible in its totality is God speaking? What is it intending to say? Is there unity in this message in the entire book? It contains poetry, history, prophecy and instruction. Is all of this God speaking? What is behind the stories, the histories, the interventions of God?

These are important questions, and the starting point to answer them lies in searching out the broad, overall message of the Bible. A careful reading will show a God who is involved in the events. The story begins with the creation of our world. Then God speaks to humanity, takes initiative toward us. "God has spoken" are words frequently used. It is not a person speaking for God; it is God speaking for himself.

Imagine for a moment this book is the God of heaven bringing his message to each one of us. As you read, let it inflame your interest. A good beginning would be to get an overview of the first book, Genesis, recounting the story of the creation of our world. Then skip over to the New Testament. Here the coming of Jesus Christ unfolds for us. His miraculous acts, his kindly relationships with people, his definition of himself and finally his untimely death followed by his resurrection.

The four Gospels are "the inviolate genes of the Christian faith," as Malcolm Muggeridge put it. "To the glory of these words majestic buildings were built, Bach composed, El Greco painted, St. Augustine laboured at his *City of God* and Pascal wrote his *Pensées*. And in them Bunyan found his inspiration in describing a Pilgrim's journey through the wilderness of this world."[1]

But how can we know for ourselves the answer to the far-reaching question, is this book really divine, from God himself? To begin with, the Bible itself claims to be the inspired Word of God. While these claims alone are not final proof, they are a significant body of data that cannot be ignored. An example of this logic would be in our own court systems we take into consideration as vital evidence when a person on trial declares their innocence. The Bible emphatically states in numerous ways that its words are God's words, a major fact to be considered.

48

NO ORDINARY BOOK

Obviously the Bible is not an ordinary text book or philosophic treatise such as those by Socrates or Plato. It employs the phrase "the Word of God" 394 times in the Old Testament to refer to itself, plus it uses various synonyms such as *law, statutes, precepts, commands, ordinances* and *decrees*.[2] The New Testament regularly quotes from the Old Testament as the "Word of God." Typically, the psalmist declared in 119:11, "I have hidden your word in my heart, that I might not sin against you." This 119th Psalm is a model of literary genius with an alphabetic acrostic devoting eight verses to each of the twenty-one letters in the Hebrew alphabet, a total of 176 verses. All but one or two verses refer to the "Word of God" in some form or another.

Although written by about forty authors, this extraordinary book shows a single theme, God linking to man and man's response. This thread is woven through every book from beginning to end. The earliest book was first authored about 1100 B.C. and the last one, Revelation, was finished about one hundred years after Jesus' birth. All forty authors give glimpses of a single perspective, God's will and plan for humanity.

BEETHOVEN WAS NOT "GOD-BREATHED"

The Bible describes itself this way: *"All Scripture is God-breathed, and is useful for teaching, rebuking, correcting and training in righteousness"* (2 Timothy 3:16, emphasis added).

The word *God-breathed* (or *inspired* as other versions translate it) is not to be confused with the common usage of the word, as when we say Shakespeare was inspired and wrote great plays, or Beethoven was inspired and composed great symphonies. Inspiration, in the biblical sense, is unique. God is its primary author. It refers not to the forty writers but to the words themselves that have been written. This is an important point to grasp.

God-breathed clearly tells us where the message originated. Old Testament "prophecy never had its origin in the will of man, but men spoke from God as they were *carried along* by the Holy Spirit" (2 Peter 1:21, emphasis added). The Bible is the product of God himself. These are not mere human ideas but God's divine character and will revealed through human words. Those writers of Scripture were not mere writing machines. God did not punch them, like keys on a typewriter, to produce his message. He did not dictate the words, as the biblical view of inspiration has so often been caricatured. It is quite clear that each writer had a style of his own. Jeremiah did not write like Isaiah, and John did not write like Paul. God worked through the instrumentality of human personality but so guided and controlled the people that what they wrote is *what he wanted written*.

49

INDICATION OF SUPERNATURAL ORIGIN

The Bible is the word of God regardless of one's opinion of it. Merely believing it doesn't make it true. Disbelieving it doesn't make it untrue. Throughout the entire book are intimations of the Bible's claim to a supernatural origin.

• The prophets and other writers were consciously aware that they were God's mouthpieces. *"The word of the LORD came to me"* is a phrase that recurs frequently in the Old Testament. David says, "The Spirit of the LORD spoke through me; his word was on my tongue" (2 Samuel 23:2). Jeremiah said, "The LORD reached out his hand and touched my mouth and said to me, 'Now, I have put my words in your mouth'" (Jeremiah 1:9).

Then when later writers of Scripture quoted parts of the Scripture that had previously been recorded, they frequently quoted them as words spoken by God rather than by a particular prophet. For instance, Paul writes, "The Scripture foresaw that God would justify the Gentiles by faith, and announced the gospel in advance to Abraham: 'All nations will be blessed through you'" (Galatians 3:8).

• God was spoken of in some passages as if he *were* the Scriptures. For example, "Sovereign Lord, . . . you spoke by the Holy Spirit through the mouth of your servant, our father David: 'Why do the nations rage and the peoples plot in vain?'" (Acts 4:24-25 quoting Psalm 2:1). Benjamin Warfield points out the dual fact that in some instances Scripture is spoken of as if they were God and others spoke as if God himself were the Scriptures. This could only result from a habitual identification in the mind of the writers that the text of Scripture *was God speaking*. It became natural, then, to use the phrase "Scripture said" and to use the phrase "God says" when what was really intended was, "Scripture, the Word of God, says. . . ." The two sets of passages, together, thus show an absolute identification of Scripture with the speaking God.[3]

• The New Testament writers were equally clear in their claim to have the same prophetic authority as Old Testament writers. Jesus said John the Baptist was a prophet and more than a prophet (Matthew 11:9-15). As Gordon Clark has put it, "The New Testament prophets were no less inspired than their Old Testament forerunners."[4]

Paul claims prophetic authority: "If anybody thinks he is a prophet or spiritually gifted, let him acknowledge that what I am writing to you is the Lord's command" (1 Corinthians 14:37).

Peter speaks of Paul's letters as that "which ignorant and unstable people distort, as they do the other Scriptures, to their own destruction" (2 Peter 3:16). His reference to them on the same level as "the other Scriptures" shows that he viewed them as having the prophetic authority of Scripture.

JESUS' VIEW OF SCRIPTURE

Most significant of all, however, is Jesus' view of the Scripture. What did he think of it? How did he use it? If we can answer these questions, we have the answer from the incarnate Word of God himself, the One about whom the Bible spoke.

Jesus' attitude was transparently open about the Old Testament. He states emphatically, "I tell you the truth, until heaven and earth disappear, not the smallest letter, not the least stroke of a pen, will by any means disappear from the Law until everything is accomplished" (Matthew 5:18). He quoted Scripture as final authority, often introducing the statement with the phrase, "It is written," as in his encounter with Satan in the temptation in the wilderness (Matthew 4). After the resurrection he spoke of himself and of events surrounding his life as being fulfillments of the Scripture:

> How then would the Scriptures be fulfilled that say it must happen in this way? . . . But this has all taken place that the writings of the prophets might be fulfilled. (Matthew 26:54-56)

When Jesus first started teaching, he sat in the synagogue in Nazareth where he grew up. An attendant handed him a scroll of the prophet Isaiah. Jesus unrolled the scroll and began to read the eight-hundred-year-old document. He read Isaiah 61:1-2, gave it back to the attendant and sat down. Every eye was fixed on him, intent on his next words, which were *"Today this scripture is fulfilled in your hearing."*

Imagine the electricity after he announced he had fulfilled a prophecy written eight hundred years previously. Luke records, "All ... were amazed at the gracious words that came from his lips" (Luke 4:22). The watching crowd wanted him to do miracles. Yet they felt a restraining reverence for him as he read these words:

> The Spirit of the Lord is on me,
>> because he has anointed me
>> to preach good news to the poor.
> He has sent me to proclaim freedom for the prisoners
>> and recovery of sight for the blind,
> to release the oppressed,
>> to proclaim the year of the Lord's favor.
> (Luke 4:18-19)

Perhaps his most sweeping endorsement and acceptance of the Old Testament was when he declared with finality, *"The Scripture cannot be broken"* (John 10:35, emphasis added).

If, then, we acknowledge Jesus Christ as Savior and Lord, it would be a contradiction in terms, and strangely inconsistent, if we rejected the Scripture as the Word of God. This would find us in disagreement with the One Savior whom we acknowledge to be the eternal God, the Creator of the universe.

Some have suggested that in Jesus' view of the Old Testament, he

51

accommodated himself to the prejudices of his contemporary hearers. In other words, he went along with his culture's views on some issues. The theory is, since the teachers in the synagogues accepted it as authoritative, he appealed to the Old Testament to gain wider acceptance for his teaching.

As the Nazareth incident above shows, grave difficulties beset this thesis. Jesus' recognition and use of the authority of the Old Testament was not superficial or peripheral. It continued to be the heart of his teaching concerning his person and work. Otherwise he would be guilty of grave deception in his teaching. Moreover, why would he accommodate himself in some points and not on others? This is doubtless an untenable position.

HELPFUL DEFINITIONS

Several definitions can illumine our understanding of the Bible as the Word of God.

Is accepting the Bible as the Word of God the same as taking the entire Bible literally? The question "Do you believe the Bible literally?" is like the question "Have you stopped beating your wife?" Either a yes or a no answer convicts the one who responds. Whenever the question is asked, the term *literal* needs to be carefully defined.

A "literal view" of the Bible does not mean we do not recognize figures of speech used in Scripture. When Isaiah said "the trees of the field will clap their hands" (Isaiah 55:12), and the psalmist said "mountains skipped like rams" (Psalm 114:4, 6), no rational reading of these figures would view these in literal terms. There is poetry, prose and other literary forms used. A literal view interprets any passage in the sense the authors intended it to be received by readers. This is the same principle one employs when reading the newspaper, where it is remarkably easy to distinguish between figures of speech and those statements a writer intends his readers to take literally—especially on the sports pages!

By contrast, if we do not take the Bible literally, we can easily evade the clear intent of the authors. Such a view would take certain biblical events (for instance, the Fall of humanity or miracles) as nonfactual stories recorded only to illustrate and convey spiritual truth.

Those holding this view would say that it compares to the saying, "Don't kill the goose that lays the golden egg." Its truth does not hinge on the literal factuality of the existence of a goose or a golden egg in Aesop's fable. Then, this view says we need not insist on the historicity of biblical events and records to enjoy and realize the truth they convey. Some writers have applied this principle even to the cross and the resurrection of Jesus Christ. The expression "taking the Bible literally," therefore is ambiguous and must be carefully defined to avoid great confusion.

To summarize, first, the application of this logic evades the clear intent of the words grammatically and syntactically. It misses the overall unity beginning in Genesis with God's covenant to deliver "all the world" and fulfilling it literally in Jesus Christ. Second, to apply this principle leaves biblical events such as the cross and the resurrection of Jesus Christ as merely nonfactual stories of no importance. Third, this view leads to a subjective pick-and-choose interpretation removing any thought of divine biblical inspiration. The expression "taking the Bible literally," therefore, is ambiguous and must be carefully defined to aid understanding.

"The Bible is inerrant" is another important teaching that needs to be carefully defined. What does *inerrancy* mean and what does it not mean? This too can be misunderstood. A general definition: In the original manuscripts, the thoughts God wanted written were written. The words the writers used were guarded by God.

• Twentieth-century standards of scientific, historical precision and accuracy on the biblical writers does not hold true for any ancient writings. For instance, the Scripture describes things phenomenologically—that is, as they appear to be, even as they appear to us. It speaks of the sun rising and setting. Of course, we know that the sun doesn't actually rise and set but that the earth rotates. We use sunrise and sunset, even in an age of scientific enlightenment, because this is a convenient way of describing *what appears to be happening.* Consequently, we cannot charge the Bible with error when it speaks phenomenologically. It speaks in this way, as have people of all ages and cultures.

• The same standards of exactness in historical matters were not used in ancient times. Although

> **God's revelation is designed to make us Christians, not scientists!**
>
> • **He made everything.**
>
> • **He made everything out of nothing.**
>
> • **He made everything good.**

illustrations abound of the wars, dynasties and reigns of kings in the Bible, round numbers were used rather than precise figures. Today we also do this. When the police estimate a crowd, we know the figure is not precise but close enough for their purpose.

• Some apparent errors may be errors in transcription when hand copying the texts. Gutenberg invented the printing press and printed the first Bible in Latin in the 1450s. Although tedious, hand copying had been the method used previously to make Bibles during the centuries before Gutenberg. Remarkably, evidence has demonstrated the overall accuracy of the text from copy to copy over time with very minor mistakes due to the utmost care given each copy.

In comparing these thousands of biblical documents, some problems as yet do not yield a ready explanation. We can freely admit this, remembering many times in the past when possible discrepancies in a text were resolved when more data became available. Therefore, the logical position would be, where there are areas of seeming contradictions, to hold the problem in abeyance. We can admit our present inability to explain and await the possibility of new data. The presence of problems does not prevent us from accepting the Bible as the supernatural Word of God.

E. J. Carnell illustrates from science:

> There is a close parallel between science and Christianity which surprisingly few seem to notice. As Christianity *assumes* that all in the Bible is supernatural, so the scientist *assumes* that all in nature is rational and orderly. Both are hypotheses based, not on all of the evidence, but on the evidence "for the most part."
>
> Science devoutly holds to the hypothesis that all of nature is mechanical, though, as a matter of fact, the mysterious electron keeps jumping around as expressed by what is called *the Heisenberg principle of uncertainty.*
>
> How does science justify its hypothesis that all of nature is mechanical, when it admits on other grounds many areas of nature do not seem to conform to this pattern? The answer is that since regularity is observed in nature "for the most part," the smoothest hypothesis is to assume that it is the same throughout the whole.[5]

ASTONISHING PROPHECIES

A further confirmation that the Bible is the Word of God is in the remarkable number of fulfilled prophecies it contains.

These prophecies are not vague generalities like those given by modern fortunetellers: "A handsome man/woman will soon come into your life." Such predictions are susceptible to easy misinterpretation. Many Bible prophecies are specific in their details, and the authentication and veracity of the prophet rests on them. The Scripture itself makes it clear that fulfilled prophecy is one of the evidences of the supernatural origin of the word of its prophets (Jeremiah 28:9).

Failure of fulfillment would unmask a false prophet. Deuteronomy says: "You may say to yourselves, 'How can we know when a message has not been spoken by the LORD?' If what a prophet proclaims in the name of the LORD does not take place or come true, that is a message the LORD has not spoken. That prophet has spoken presumptuously. Do not be afraid of him" (Deuteronomy 18:21-22).

Isaiah also ties the unmasking of false prophets to the failure of their predictive prophecy. "Bring in your idols to tell us what is going to happen. Tell us what the former things were, so that we may consider them and know their final outcome. Or declare to us the things to come, tell us what the future holds, so we may know that you are gods. Do something, whether good or bad, so that we will be dismayed and filled with fear" (Isaiah 41:22-23).

Three kinds of prophecies are seen in the Old Testament:

• *Predictions of a coming Messiah, the Lord Jesus Christ, are incredibly detailed.* The early disciples quoted the Old Testament prophecies regularly to show that Jesus fulfilled in detail the prophecies made hundreds of years earlier. Many of these were written by these prophets five hundred to one thousand years before Christ came to earth. The kind of specific detail given is unequalled in any other major religion of the world.

We can mention only a small but representative number of the prophecies. Jesus referred to the predictive prophecies about himself in what must have been one of the most exciting Bible studies in history. After a conversation with two disciples as they walked toward Emmaus, he said, "'How slow of heart to believe all that the prophets have spoken! Did not the Christ have to suffer these things and then enter his glory?' And beginning with Moses and all the Prophets, he explained to them what was said in all the Scriptures concerning himself" (Luke 24:25-27).

Isaiah 52:13—53:12 is the most outstanding example of predictive prophecy about Christ. Its contingencies could not have been rigged in advance in an attempt to produce fulfillment. Fifteen specific words or phrases can be found in these verses that fit his life exactly. They involve his life and his rejection in ministry, his death, his burial and his reactions to the unjust judicial proceedings. These were written eight hundred years before Jesus lived!

Micah 5:2 is a striking illustration of both a prediction about Christ and historic detail: "But you, Bethlehem Ephrathah, though you are small among the clans of Judah, out of you will come for me one who will be ruler over Israel, whose origins are from of old, from ancient times."

It took a decree from the mighty Caesar Augustus himself to have a census taken, bringing Mary and Joseph from Nazareth to Bethlehem Ephrathah where Jesus was born. The designation of Ephrathah was given because there was a second Bethlehem north of this one. The Scripture was fulfilled exactly!

The New Testament contains thirty-eight references to Isaiah 53 and twenty-four references to Psalm 22.[6]

56

Event in Jesus' Life	Old Testament	Fulfilled Prophecy
Born in Bethlehem	Micah 5:2	Luke 2:4-7
Sold for thirty pieces of silver	Zechariah 1:13	Matthew 26:15
Silver used to buy a potter's field	Zechariah 11:13	Matthew 27:6
Silent when accused	Isaiah 53:7	Matthew 27:12-14
Condemned with criminals	Isaiah 53:12	Luke 23:32-33
Raging thirst when dying	Psalm 22:15	John 19:28
Silent when accused	Isaiah 53:7	Matthew 27:12-14
Crucified [hands and feet pierced]	Psalm 22:16	John 19:18
Pierced after death	Isaiah 53:5	Luke 23:46
Buried by a rich man	Isaiah 53:9	Matthew 27:57-60
Suffering not the end	Isaiah 53:11	Luke 24:1-8

Table 5.1. Events predicted and fulfilled in Jesus' life

• *There are predictions dealing with kings, nations and cities.* A most remarkable one has to do with the city of Tyre in Ezekiel 26. Here details are given as to how Tyre would be destroyed, the utter completeness of its destruction, and the fact that it would never be reconstructed (v. 4). How this prophecy was fulfilled in stages through Nebuchadnezzar's attack and then through the savage onslaught of Alexander the Great is a phenomenal illustration of the accuracy and reality of predictive prophecy in the Bible.

• *There are predictions about the Jewish people, the Israelites.* Again, only a few of these startling prophecies will be cited.

Their dispersion to conquering nations was predicted by Moses and Hosea. "The LORD will cause you to be defeated before your enemies. You will come at them from one direction but flee from them in seven, and you will become a thing of horror to all the kingdoms on earth" (Deuteronomy 28:25). "My God will reject them because they have not obeyed him; they will be wanderers among the nations" (Hosea 9:17). Jeremiah 31 makes the astonishing prediction of the restoration of Israel as a nation. For centuries this was considered unthinkable. Some events in our own time, however, may well be at least partial fulfillment of these prophecies. All observers agree that the reestablishment of Israel as a nation in 1948 is one of the amazing political phenomena of our day.

One cannot deny the force of fulfilled prophecy as evidence of divine guidance. Furthermore, these are prophecies which could not possibly have been schemed and written after the events predicted (see table 5.1 above).

57

GOD SPEAKS THROUGH HIS BOOK

There are, then, a number of pieces of evidence on which one can reasonably base his or her belief that the Bible is the Word of God. As one reads, the confirmation of the Holy Spirit is what finally turns doubt into belief that the Bible is the Word of God. As a person views the evidence and reads the Bible, "it dawns on him," to use Gordon Clark's phrase, that the Bible is the Word of God.[7] This realization is the work of God's Holy Spirit and is never trivial but always toward some purpose. As one reads, the mind is enlightened, the heart is touched and there comes a convincing discernment of the Scripture's message.

After their conversation with the risen Christ, the two disciples on the road to Emmaus asked, "Were not our hearts burning within us?" (Luke 24:32). This same experience becomes ours as, with the Holy Spirit's help, we come to the conviction that the Bible is the Word of God. We feed on it and through it we are brought into the presence of the divine Author himself.

FOR FURTHER READING

Lewis, C. S. "Modern Theology and Biblical Criticism," in *Christian Reflections*. Grand Rapids, Mich.: Eerdmans; London: Geoffrey Bles, 1994.

Van Buren, Paul M. *According to the Scriptures: The Origin of the Gospel and of the Church's Old Testament*. Grand Rapids, Mich.: Eerdmans, 1998.

CHAPTER SIX

ARE THE BIBLE
DOCUMENTS RELIABLE?

Several years ago a national magazine carried an article purporting to show that there are thousands of errors in the Bible. The question then arises: How do we know that the text of the Bible as we have it today, having come to us through many translations and versions over the centuries, is not just a pale reflection of the original? What guarantee do we have that deletions and embellishments have not totally obscured the original message of the Bible? What difference does the historical accuracy of the Bible make? Surely the only thing that counts is the message!

But Christianity is rooted in history. Jesus Christ was counted in a Roman census. If the Bible's historical references are not true, grave questions may be raised. Also, are the *spiritual parts* of its message true, encased as they are in historical events? Are the books now included in the Bible substantially the same documents the people had two thousand years ago? How do we know whether other books should have been included? These questions and others are worthy of answers.

In finding the answers to this litany of questions, let us first remind ourselves of the primary truths we are building on from the previous chapters.

• There is a rational body of truth for belief in God and in Jesus Christ. No need to kiss our brains good-bye.

• God exists and is a personal, knowable God. He desires to communicate with us, his creation.

• God has come to earth in the incarnation and resurrection of Jesus Christ to establish this relationship with us.

• God has used the medium of words, the Bible, to reveal himself, his character and his plan.

Now we turn to examining this book for its credentials and reliability. The Bible describes events covering many generations, and the texts were written by some forty authors. The accuracy and truthfulness of these accounts is of paramount importance, and the process of establishing the accuracy is no small task. Examining the sixty-six books and their origins is called the science of textual criticism. It has to do with the reliability of the text, that is, how our current text compares with the originals and how accurately the ancient manuscripts were copied.

BEFORE THE PRINTING PRESS

The ancient manuscripts, of course, had no pages as we have now. For the Old Testament, clay and wooden tablets predominated. Reed papyrus and parchment skins were also used and rolled into scrolls. Pottery pieces and even beaten metal fragments have been found. No ink is mentioned but only an iron stylus or a reed pen sharpened with a penknife. Since not everyone could read or had a scroll, a high premium was placed on the public reading and hearing of the documents. This helps our understanding of the emphasis on "hearing the word of the LORD" in the Old Testament.[1]

It wasn't until around A.D. 1456 that Gutenberg created the first moveable type printing press and printed his first book, the Bible in Latin. From then on, access to books and the reading of them began to proliferate.

The work of the "scribes" or "copyists" with the scrolls was a highly professional and carefully executed task. For the Hebrews, it was undertaken by devout Jews with the highest dedication. Since they believed they were dealing with the Word of God, they were acutely aware of the need for extreme care and accuracy. Their devotion is seen in habits like wiping a pen clean before writing the name of God, copying one letter at a time, counting the *letters* of both the original and the one copied. In some cases, when discrepancies were found, the entire copy was destroyed.

The earliest and most widely used *complete* copy of the entire Hebrew Old Testament is from around A.D. 900. Called the Masoretic text, it is the product of able Jewish scribes known as the Masoretes (literally "transmitters"), custodians of the Hebrew text from A.D. 500 to 1000. The Hebrew text of the Old Testament used today is called the Masoretic text, validating the quality of the work done more than a thousand years ago. All of the present copies of the Hebrew text we have today are in remarkable agreement with this text. Copying and proofreading was indeed a skillful art. Confirmation of the accuracy of a text is checked by comparing it with the Latin and Greek copies from the same time period.

THE DEAD SEA SCROLLS

In 1947 the world learned about what has been called the greatest archaeological discovery of the century. In caves in the valley of the Dead Sea, ancient jars were discovered containing the now-famous Dead Sea Scrolls. From these scrolls it is evident that a group of dedicated Jews lived at a place near the Dead Sea called Qumran from about 150 B.C. to A.D. 70.

Benefits from the Scrolls

• They confirmed the accuracy of one thousand years of both the record and the history of the Hebrews—that is, from 200 B.C. to A.D. 916.

• The scrolls' translation and the official text used in the Jerusalem temple reinforce each other's accuracy above all other manuscripts.

• The extensive evidence found strengthens our confidence in the histories previously uncovered. As a result, earlier copies of the Pentateuch and histories also have a high probability of accuracy.

61

Qumran was a communal society, operated very much like a monastery. In addition to tilling the fields they spent their time studying and copying the Scriptures. It became apparent to them in A.D. 70 that the Romans were coming to invade the land. Their leather scrolls were put in jars and hidden in the caves of cliffs on the west side of the Dead Sea.

In the providence of God the scrolls survived undisturbed until discovered accidentally by a young Bedouin goat herdsman in February or March 1947. This discovery was followed by careful exploration of the area, yielding a total of eleven other caves containing scrolls. The find included the earliest manuscript copy yet known of the complete book of Isaiah, and another one contained about one-third of the book. Later discoveries brought *fragments of every book in the Old Testament* except the book of Esther.

In addition, there is a fragmented copy containing much of Isaiah 38—66. The books of Samuel, in a tattered copy, were also found at that time, along with two complete chapters of Habakkuk. A number of nonbiblical items, including the rules of the ancient community, were also found.

The significance of this find, for those who question the accuracy of the Old Testament text, can easily be seen. In one dramatic stroke *almost one thousand years were bridged,* closing the gap in the age of the manuscripts we now possess. It would be similar to being told that a painting you owned is not two hundred but a thousand years old. Enthusiastic comparing of these Dead Sea Scrolls with the Masoretic text resulted in discovering remarkable accuracy of the transmission process. A period of nearly a millennium was closed.

What was actually learned? Comparison between the Qumran manuscript of Isaiah 38—66 with the one we had gives an exciting picture. Scholars found:

> The text is extremely close to our Masoretic text. A comparison of Isaiah 53 shows that only seventeen letters differ from the Masoretic text. Ten of these are mere differences of spelling, like our "honor" or "honour" and produce no change in the meaning at all. Four others are very minor differences, such as the presence of the conjunction, which is often a matter of style. The other three letters are the Hebrew word for "light" which is added after "they shall see" in verse 11. Out of 166 words in this chapter, only this one word is really in question, and it does not at all change the sense of the passage. This is typical of the whole manuscript.[2]

THREE IMPORTANT VERSIONS

The Hebrew people migrated throughout eastern Asia due to travel and wars. Other scrolls have been found from Egypt to Rome.

Comparing these with each other has fortified our confidence in the historicity of the events earlier in the Old Testament.

• The *Septuagint,* meaning "seventy," is a Greek translation of the Old Testament and is the oldest and most important. The expansion of the Jewish people into the whole of the Middle East as well as the coming of Alexander the Great from Greece around 250 B.C. Hellenized the culture. Consequently, many Jewish people knew no Hebrew, only Greek, and failed to participate in the temple worship. Referred to as the LXX, translated by seventy-two Jewish scholars in the third century B.C., this Greek translation became a bridge for understanding the Hebrew history and theology in the Old Testament.

• The *Syriac version* written in the Aramaic language of Syria is the oldest and most important translation after the Septuagint. It continued in use with some revisions from the Septuagint.

• The *Samaritan version* is another ancient account similar to the others. This one contains copies of the Hebrew Pentateuch, the term applied to the first five books of the Old Testament. Unquestionably it is derived from the split between the Jerusalem Jews and the Samaritans. Copies of the old scrolls of the Pentateuch are extant today in Nablus (Shechem), Palestine.

These and other types of texts existed in 200 B.C. We can conclude with R. Laird Harris:

63

> We can now be sure that copyists worked with great care and accuracy on the Old Testament, even back to 225 B.C. Although some differed among themselves, it was so little, we can infer that still earlier copyists had also faithfully and carefully transmitted the Old Testament text. Indeed, it would be rash skepticism that would now deny that we have our Old Testament in a form very close to that used by Ezra when he taught the Law to those who had returned from the Babylonian captivity—about B.C. 457 (Ezra 9—10).[3]

NEW TESTAMENT DOCUMENTS

Not more than one-thousandth part of the whole New Testament is affected by differences of reading. This was the conclusion of the great scholar F. J. A. Hort from a lifetime of studying early documentary evidence. He added that in the New Testament there were only insignificant variations in grammar or spelling between various documents.[4]

Originally written in Greek, the latest number of manuscripts now known tops 5,500; some are complete and some are very small fragments. One of these fragments has been determined to be the very earliest of all known pieces. It comes from John 18 and has only five verses—three on one side and two on the other—about the size of a 3 x 5 card. Because this fragment came from Egypt and was copied and circulated from Patmos, Asia Minor, where the apostle John was exiled, a group of scholars estimated it must have been composed (at least) by A.D. 90–100.[5]

Unlike the Old Testament, the New Testament was written with ink and pen, mostly on papyrus (from the plant) or parchment (animal skin). References to the ink are made in 2 John 12 and 3 John 13. Also, the apostle Paul makes a poignant request in a letter to his friends to bring him a cloak he had left behind "and my scrolls, especially the parchments." It is assumed the parchments he mentioned were the Old Testament on animal skins (2 Timothy 4:13).

The flood of documentary evidence brings us to ask when the New Testament was written. The crucifixion of Jesus Christ took place, it is generally agreed, about A.D. 30. This is has been carefully compared with the dates of the ruling emperor, Tiberius Caesar, along with other Roman hierarchy, according to F. F. Bruce. The New Testament was complete or substantially complete about A.D. 100. This means that the majority of the writing had been done before this by contemporaries of Christ who saw, heard and remembered what he said and did.[6]

The time elapsing between the actual events and the writing of the books, from the standpoint of historical research is satisfactorily short. Some of the Pauline letters are even earlier than some of the Gospels. Again, based on the evidence, the text we read today does not differ in any substantial way from the originals as it came from the hands of the human writer.[7]

The extraordinary number of copies of early New Testament materials defies imagination. When we compare it with other documents of ancient writings from the same time, it fills us

F. F. Bruce says that there is no body of ancient literature in the world that enjoys such a wealth of good textual attestation as the New Testament.

with admiration. For the New Testament there are two excellent manuscripts from the fourth century A.D. Fragments of papyrus copies of books of the New Testament date from one hundred to two hundred years earlier still. Bruce again says that there is no body of ancient literature in the world that enjoys such a wealth of good textual attestation as the New Testament.[8] By contrast, among the works of classical writers, contemporaries of Christ, no one questions the existence of these secular authors or the validity of their writings. Have you ever heard anyone ask, "How do we know Socrates ever lived?" Yet there is far less supportive documentary evidence for his and other contemporary Greek and Latin writers than of the New Testament and its account. The four Gospels, twenty-one letters, the history of Acts and visions of Revelation have a manuscript attestation second to none and superior to most. See table 6.1 for a comparison of numbers and dates.[9]

Writer/Earliest Known Manuscript	Date of Writer	Number of Manuscripts
Thucycides/1,300 yrs after he lived	460-400 B.C.	9
Aristotle (*Poetics*)/1,400 yrs after he lived	343 B.C.	5
Caesar (*Gallic Wars*)/900 yrs after he lived	58-50 B.C.	9-10

Table 6.1. Dates and number of manuscripts by secular writers

ADDITIONAL CONFIRMATION

Other sources support the authenticity of the New Testament, particularly as the church spread. References and quotations of the New Testament books were used by both friends and enemies of Christianity. The early church leaders who wrote mostly between A.D. 90 and 160 give indication of familiarity with most of the books of the New Testament. Also the Gnostic school of Valentinus (scholars searching for salvation through knowledge) was familiar with most of the New Testament.[10]

• *Versions* are those manuscripts translated from the Greek into other languages. In addition to the Syriac versions, there were the

Egyptian or Coptic versions and Latin versions. Fragments of papyrus copies of books of the New Testament date from the fourth century A.D. and earlier. By careful study of these versions important clues have been uncovered as to the original Greek manuscripts from which they were translated.

• *Lectionaries,* the reading lessons used in public church services, are another source. More than 1,800 of these reading lessons have been classified. There are lectionaries of the Gospels, the Acts and the Epistles. Though they did not appear before the sixth century, the texts from which they quote are generally early and of high quality. Though there have been many changes in the many copyings of the New Testament writings, most of them are minor. The trustworthiness of our New Testament text deserves our informed respect.

When we are confronted with published accounts of biblical "errors," we can rest with the conclusion of the late Sir Frederic Kenyon, a world-renowned scholar of the ancient manuscripts:

66

> The interval, then, between the dates of original composition and the earliest extant evidence becomes so small as to be in fact negligible, and the last foundation for any doubt that the Scriptures have come down to us substantially as they were written has now been removed. Both the authenticity and the general integrity of the books of the New Testament may be regarded as finally established.[11]

"The Word of God is like a lion. You don't have to defend a lion. All you have to do is let the lion loose, and the lion will defend itself."

Charles Spurgeon

THE QUESTION OF THE CANON

A question closely allied to that of the reliability of the texts we have is, How do we know the books in our Bible, and no others, are the ones that should be there? This is called the question of the canon, or the list of books seen as inspired by God. There are distinct questions involved for Old and New Testaments.

The thirty-nine books of the Hebrew Bible are divided into three groups:

• *The Law:* Genesis to Deuteronomy, which are the first five books of the Bible, also called the Torah or Pentateuch

• *The Prophets:* "Former Prophets" (Joshua, Judges, 1-2 Samuel, 1-2 Kings), "Latter Prophets" (Isaiah, Jeremiah, Ezekiel) and "The Book of the Twelve" (Hosea to Malachi)

• *The Writings:* the remaining books of our Old Testament canon (Ruth, 1-2 Chronicles, Ezra, Nehemiah, Esther, Job, Psalms, Proverbs, Song of Solomon, Ecclesiastes, Lamentations, Daniel)

The Protestant Bible includes the same Old Testament books that the Jews approved and Jesus and the apostles accepted. The Roman Catholic Church includes the books of the Apocrypha since the Council of Trent in 1546. The order in the English Bible follows that of the Septuagint.

The books were received as authoritative because they were recognized as utterances of people inspired by God to reveal his Word. As E. J. Young says:

> When the Word of God was written, it became Scripture, and as it had been spoken by God, it possessed his absolute authority. Therefore, it was the Word of God and was canonical. That which determines the canonicity of a book, therefore, is the fact that the book is inspired of God.[12]

We can see this development in the work of Moses. The laws issued by him and the latter prophets were intended to be respected as the decrees of God himself. They and succeeding generations saw it as from God. The Law was neglected at times by the nation of Israel, but its authority was recognized by her spiritual leaders. This profound recognition shook Josiah when he realized how long the Law had been neglected: "When the king [Josiah] heard the words of the Book of the Law, he tore his robes" (2 Kings 22:11).

By the beginning of the Christian era the term *Scripture* had come to mean a fixed body of divinely inspired writings that were fully recognized as authoritative. It is interesting that there was no controversy between Jesus and the Pharisees on the authority of the Old Testament. Contention arose because the Pharisees placed tradition on the same level as the authority of Scripture. To some degree, we need to be aware when tradition rears it head for controversy today. The basis for faith today can be differentiated between truth and merely tradition.

The church Council of Jamnia, in A.D. 90, held informal discussions about the canon. Whether any formal or binding decisions were made is problematic. However, there was a firm confirmation at a church council in Carthage in A.D. 397 when the New Testament canon was fixed.

THE APOCRYPHAL BOOKS

The apocryphal (meaning "hidden") books, were twelve books never received into the Jewish canon. They were not considered as part of the inspired Scriptures by Jews or Christians in the early centuries of the Christian era. This is evident from a study of the writings of Josephus, the Jewish historian, and of Augustine, the great North African Bishop of Hippo. It is noteworthy that the New Testament writers do not once quote the Apocrypha.

The Apocryphal books themselves do not claim to be the Word of God or the work of the prophets. They vary greatly in content and value, giving some helpful historical background. Though not included at first, these books were later added to the Septuagint, then came to be included by Jerome in the Latin Vulgate in the early fifth century. Even Jerome, however, accepted only the books in the Hebrew Canon. Later on, in Reformation times, the Roman Catholic Church at the Council of Trent elevated the Apocrypha to canonical status.

For the Old Testament we have, ultimately, the witness of Jesus to the canonicity of the thirty-nine books we now have.

THE NEW TESTAMENT CANON

The twenty-nine books in the New Testament were received as part of the canon by virtue of their inspiration, not by vote. Much of the material of the New Testament claimed apostolic authority. Paul and Peter clearly wrote with this authority in mind. Peter specifically refers to Paul's letters as Scripture (2 Peter 3:1-16).

Jude (v. 18) says that 2 Peter 3:3 is a word from the apostles. Such early church fathers as Polycarp, Ignatius and Clement mention a number of the New Testament books as authoritative.

The final fixation of the canon as we know it today came in the fourth century. In a letter by Athanasius in A.D. 367 he distinguishes between works in the canon, which are described as the sole sources of religious instruction, and others, which believers were permitted to

68

read. In the same year the final canon was fixed by decision of a church council held at Carthage.

Three criteria were generally used throughout this period of time to establish the particular written documents that were the true record of the voice and message of apostolic witness.

• *Was the book authored by an apostle?* The Gospels of Mark and Luke do not meet this criterion specifically but were accepted as the works of close associates of the apostles.

• *Was the book widely recognized by the church?* This centered on the matter of ecclesiastical usage. Were these canonical books used by the church or a majority of the churches?

• *Was the teaching of the book in conformity to standards of sound doctrine preached in the churches?*

These data are helpful and interesting, but in the final analysis, as with the question of the inspiration of the Scripture, canonicity is a question of the witness of God to each individual confirming the truth in the hearts of those who read it.

In days of uncertainty the Scriptures and character of the One who inspired them give us a firm rock on which to stand, intellectually and spiritually! "Heaven and earth will pass away," says the Lord God, "but my words will never pass away" (Luke 21:33).

69

FOR FURTHER READING

Bruce, F. F. *The New Testament Documents: Are They Reliable?* Downers Grove, Ill.: InterVarsity Press, 1981.

————. *The Canon of Scripture.* Downers Grove, Ill.: InterVarsity Press, 1988.

Lewis, C. S. "Modern Theology and Biblical Criticism," in *Christian Reflections.* Grand Rapids, Mich.: Eerdmans, 1994.

Wegner, Paul D. *The Origin and Development of the Bible.* Grand Rapids, Mich.: Baker, 1999.

CHAPTER SEVEN

DOES ARCHAEOLOGY VERIFY SCRIPTURE?

In the early years of the nineteenth century, a new door of information opened to uncover the earliest roots of the human race in the Near East. Increased travel and exploration provided the hinges to the door, and modern archaeologists walked through in a spurt of enthusiasm. They began to dig below the earth's surface for the material remains of humankind's past found in ancient palaces, buried temples and animal stables.

Civilizations came alive that existed long before the known world of Greece. Babylon (called "great"), where Daniel lived, revealed double walls with nine ornamented gates. Egypt showed marvels of painted tombs, bandaged mummies, mirrors, perfume jars and mascara pots.

At first the buried cultures themselves were the objects of study. Then there appeared places and names from the Old Testament on the palace walls. Names of Assyrian tyrants who warred with Israel, along with their armies and hapless captives, were found. Persian governors spoke through their letters. The Pharaohs of Egypt, some lying in solid gold coffins, could now be identified.

In the wake of these discoveries biblical scholars found rich background for the biblical history of Israel and its neighbors. The historical and geographic reliability of the Bible was affirmed in a number of important areas. This was in marked contrast to the centuries before when there was little evidence to corroborate the Bible's historical statements. Critics would dismiss the narratives by casting them as implausible stories set in fictional backgrounds rather than historical events.

By the middle of the twentieth century it began to be recognized that archaeological discoveries were substantiating the biblical record. Enlightening statements of well-known secular scholars helped affirm this. W. F. Albright of Johns Hopkins University states, "There can be no doubt that archaeology has confirmed the substantial historicity of Old Testament tradition."[1] Likewise, Millar Burrows of Yale University offers this endorsement:

> On the whole, however, archaeological work has unquestionably strengthened confidence in the reliability of the scriptural record. More than one archaeologist has found his respect for the Bible increased by the experience of excavation in Palestine. Archaeology has in many cases refuted the views of modern critics. It has shown, in a number of instances, that these views rest on false assumptions and unreal, artificial schemes of historical development. This is a real contribution and not to be minimized.[2]

72

BIBLICAL HISTORY CONFIRMED

The help from archaeology covers several categories.

• Some *specific biblical events* previously doubted and even ridiculed have been verified. The impact of this is shown in the observation of one scholar that it is a rare biblical passage that has not been questioned by someone.

• *The overall background* of the culture and practices in general of the biblical times was filled in. Such things as economic problems and literary development describe the world to which the Old Testament prophets spoke.

• *Some points of apparent conflict between the biblical record and the information previously available have been surprisingly cleared up* as more information has been obtained. It would seem, then, that when apparent conflicts still exist, rather than conclude that the Bible must be wrong, a more reasonable position would be to admit the problem exists and to hold it open pending further discoveries.

Having said all this, however, our point of reference is always that we cannot prove the Bible by archaeology, nor do we believe the Bible

Archaeology confirms the biblical accounts in more than 25,000 sites connected to biblical history.

on the basis of archaeological proof. H. Darnel Lance writes to this: "Although archaeology can sometimes provide independent evidence for the existence of certain places, persons or events mentioned in the Bible, it can say nothing at all about whether God had anything to do with any of it. That, for the modern believer as well as for the ancient Israelite, is a matter of faith."[3]

Added to faith, it is God who ultimately confirms the spiritual truth of the Scripture as we read it. Archaeology confirms the accounts recorded. Spiritual truth comes from God himself. The historical details repeatedly confirmed by archaeology inspire our confidence to look beyond the historical events to "the Story of God"—*Story* with a capital S, as Leighton Ford expresses it.[4]

SOURCES OF ARCHAEOLOGISTS

More than 25,000 sites showing some connection with the Old Testament period have been located in Bible lands. Yet there is still a wealth of material that awaits discovery. Throughout the Near East mounds of earth and debris (called "tells") mark the place where towns or cities once flourished. Most of the major cities of the Bible can be identified, A. R. Milliard states, either by "general geographical considerations or by tradition (though that may not be very reliable) or by current use of the ancient name."[5]

A major example of ancient names continuing is the city of Damascus. Known to us through the apostle Paul's conversion in Acts 9, it has existed under that name for 3,500 years or more.

Ancient Eastern inscriptions from the entire Middle East give insightful comparison with the Bible. Stones, pottery, walls and other places show writings in neighboring languages. Pictures and other artifacts open up details of the cultures. Excavation of biblical sites themselves expand the information related to the stories told. They tell us how people lived, how they built houses and how they worked. Excavations have opened up whole civilizations and their actual existence and amazing skills. The field of information and correlation with biblical data is so vast that we can spotlight only a few of the major contributions.

73

HOW ARE THE FINDS DATED?

Ancient cities were built, disintegrated with time and rebuilt in the same place. Because of this a whole succession of levels is commonly found, the lowest of course, being the oldest. The question arises, How can these finds be dated?

Fashions in pottery would change in each new culture. If a particular fashion at one excavated site can be dated, a similar pottery found elsewhere would obviously be from the same period. Kings often inscribed their names on the hinge-sockets of temple doors, and the names of their gods would be given. Also, inscribed stones were often laid under palace or temple walls in memory of the founder. Royal sepulchers were identified in the same way.

Copies of lists of events and people have been uncovered dating back to almost 2000 B.C. Some were drawn up by Sumerian scribes cataloging the kings according to their successive dynasties with notes as to the lengths of their reigns. A few miles from the city of Ur, the early home of Abraham, a foundation stone was uncovered. First mentioned in Genesis 11 and 15, the stone had been laid by a king of unknown name, of the First Dynasty of Ur. Significantly, the scribes speak of this as the third dynasty after the Flood. This king apparently reigned 3,100 years before Christ and more than a thousand years before Abraham.[6]

2000 B.C.: ABRAHAM'S TIME

A good example of the help archaeology can be to us comes from the life and times of Abraham (about 2166-1991 B.C.). The discovery of three cities, Mari, Nuzi and Alalakh, opened up new information of ancient civilizations, giving clues of life in Syria and Mesopotamia historically and politically. In addition, we get a new view into the urban lifestyles of Abraham's contemporaries. This is in sharp contrast with the pastoral life known from the "Patriarchs," as the early fathers of the Bible's first five books were called.

These records cover a broad spectrum from business, politics, government and the arts. They reflect customs and social relationships that parallel the situations the biblical Patriarchs faced.

When we see Abraham in the settings similar to those known from the cities of Mari and Nuzi, the biblical accounts become highly credible and believable. The life and history, the political movements, the cultural and business activities of these cities paint a wonderfully illuminated background of the world of the father of the Hebrew nation.

In 1933 a party of Arabs was digging a grave by the upper Euphrates River just ten miles from the Iraqi border. They unearthed a stone statue and reported their find. A city named Mari was unearthed by a team of archaeologists at the site.

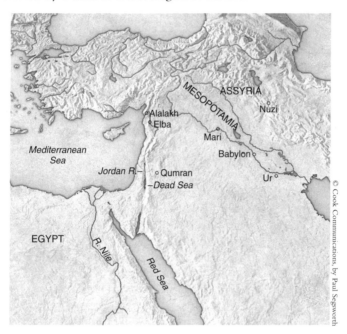

Map 7.1. Some important archaeological sites

75

They dug out more statues and eventually unearthed an elaborate palace bearing the name of the city. This was not a small royal palace. It covered more than six acres and had over 260 rooms, courtyards and passages. A. R. Millard states:

> Archaeologists usually concentrate on the more rewarding parts, where temples or palaces stood, or lay out their trenches to probe each period of existence in the life of the place. To do this a trench may slice right through the mound, producing a small amount of information at all levels.
>
> Any area of special interest can be marked and explored with a larger trench. Each building or time of occupation will have left its mark on the mound in the

form of floor surfaces, stumps of walls, and heaps of rubbish. These will be sandwiched between earlier remains below and later remains above.[7]

Millard describes the palace at Mari as containing rooms with walls fifteen feet high, some empty and some filled with jars that stood ready for oil, wine or grain. There were spacious living quarters for the king, his wives and his family; and more cramped ones for officials and servants. One can imagine craftsmen in workshops, cooks in the kitchens, secretaries, servants and singing troupes for the king's entertainment. One of the many statues found was of a bearded man dating from the eighteenth century B.C. and inscribed with the name Ishtupilum, King of Mari.[8]

Some twenty thousand cuneiform (wedge-shaped writing) tablets from royal archives were found. Accountants had used some of the tablets to record grain, vegetables and other provisions brought into the palace. Letters to the king, musical instruments and gold for decorations are all mentioned. There are even letters with messages from prophets to gods. A jar of buried treasure and inscriptions date the city around 2500 B.C.

The collection of tablets is the largest known in the literature of the ancient Middle East, containing prophesies comparable to the kinds written by Israel's prophets at the time. Since Abraham is variously thought to be in the same general era between the nineteenth and twentieth centuries B.C., this is certainly the kind of culture in which he lived.

Another city, Nuzi, situated east of the city of Mari near the Tigris River, had tablets detailing some of the social customs of the city in the fourteenth and fifteenth centuries B.C. Families are described in situations similar to the dilemma Abraham faced in Genesis 15:4 when he took Ishmael as his own son. If later the couple had a natural child, the adopted son would have to yield some of his rights to the second son. In the case of Abraham and Sarah, Isaac, Sarah's natural son, received the entire inheritance of his parents.

The Nuzi tablets recall another similar incident to Genesis 16:1-2 where Sarah presents her Egyptian handmaid, Hagar, to Abraham to bear a child because Sarah could not have children. Bible scholar Edwin M. Yamauchi tells us of a "tablet of adoption which stipulated that a barren wife must provide a slave girl to her husband to beget a son. This particular tablet and the Hammurabi Law Code requires that the slave's child be kept—a rule which was preempted by the divine command to send Hagar and Ishmael away.'"[9]

One other Syrian site, Alalakh on the Orontes River, describes wife abuse. A husband who mistreated a wife (literally "drags her by the nose") had to give up his wife, her dowry and the bridal gift presented to her family at the time of their marriage.[10]

WRITING IN THE THIRD MILLENNIUM B.C.

Did you ever wonder about the literary abilities of scribes at the time of the Old Testament patriarchs? The bustling city of Ebla provides the largest early archive thus far unearthed from the Near East. It dates back to the third millennium B.C. Although its existence had been known, its location and highly developed culture was uncertain. Archaeologists found the city was divided into two sectors, an acropolis and a lower city. The upper division contained four building complexes, including the palace of the king, temple to the goddess Ishtar and numerous stables. The lower section was divided into four quarters boasting four gates.

In a room adjacent to the temple archaeologists found an astonishing collection of thousands of tablets stacked on the floor. The small room had been burned. In the heat of the flames the brickwork was baked and the tablets as well. As a result both room and tablets withstood the ravages of the centuries until they were uncovered in 1975. History has been preserved for five thousand years![11]

Years of research will yet be required to interpret these vast records. But one of the valuable contributions of these tablets is that they provide evidence that cuneiform writing had spread to north Syria before 2300 B.C. It also shows the habit of recording every sort of activity, business and cultural. Dictionaries confirm the presence of west Semitic people of other languages in that era. Biblical history, we now know, took place in a world where writing was well established.

ISRAEL'S KINGS

Archaeology has given us colorful background information for the study of the biblical kings. Solomon's grandeur has been the target of special skepticism. His lavish wealth is described in 1 Kings 9—10 as consisting of a royal navy built on the shore of the Red Sea even though there is no suitable harbor on the coastline of Palestine. His army had use of 1,400 chariots and 1,200 horses. His building projects were extensive, including the fortification of Jerusalem, Hazor, Megiddo and Gezer (1 Kings 9:15). Recent excavation at these last three cities have at least documented Solomon's building skills.

In 1960 the famed Israeli scholar Yigael Yadin, while excavating the city of Megiddo, had identified the layer of Solomon's time by comparing pottery types. Knowing that 1 Kings 9:15 grouped together the three cities of Megiddo, Hazor and Gezer as being built by Solomon, he had a sudden inspiration. He recalled that the Megiddo Gate from Solomon's time had three chambers on each side. Could the other two cities be the same? He tells this exciting story of the dig at Hazor:

> Before proceeding further with the excavation of Hazor, we made tentative markings on the ground following our estimate of the plan of the gate on the basis of the Megiddo Gate. And then we told the laborers to go ahead and continue removing the debris. When they had finished, they looked at us with astonishment, as if we were magicians or fortunetellers. For there, before us, was the gate whose outline we had marked, a replica of the Megiddo Gate. This proved not only that both gates had been built by Solomon but that both had followed a single master plan.[12]

78

SOLOMON'S GOLD

First Kings 10:21 adds the information that Solomon possessed large stores of precious metals. The temple he built for the LORD, like the golden shrine of King Tutankhaman of Egypt, was a glory of gold as described in the latter half of 1 Kings 6. "Solomon covered the inside of the temple with pure gold, and he extended gold chains across the front of the inner sanctuary, which was overlaid with gold. So he overlaid the whole interior with gold" (6:21-22). The entire concept is breathtaking.

Although the exact site of Solomon's Temple has not been found, other discoveries showed that kings of surrounding nations of his time possessed technology and workmanship similar to the biblical account. Millard elaborates:

> Extravagant as this may seem, a display of gold was a matter of pride for any powerful ruler (i.e., valuable plates are displayed at royal banquets today). National currency reserves were held in gold, not stored idly in bank vaults to be publicized merely as figures, but

shown to the populace. When a stronger army attacked, the gold was stripped and handed over to the conquerors (cf. 2 Kings 18:16).

Assyrian, Babylonian, and Egyptian monarchs boast of the gold they donated to beautify temples in their own cities. Their inscriptions speak of walls "covered with gold like plaster," of doors and doorways carved in relief and plated with gold, of furniture and decorations sheathed in precious metal. One Assyrian king seized six decorative golden shields from a temple in Armenia, each weighing twelve times as much as each of the shields Solomon hung in his palace (1 Kings 10:1-17; cf. 14:26-27). Claims of pompous emperors may be treated as grossly inflated, but with these uses of gold that is not so. Small fragments of thin gold sheets have been found in Assyria and Babylonia, and in Egypt nail holes . . . for attaching the metal are visible in . . . stonework.[13]

At least some of Solomon's gold, we know, came from Ophir. First Kings 9:11, as well as other passages, describes Hiram, king of Tyre, as supplying Solomon "with all the cedar and pine and gold he wanted." And verse 28 tells of Hiram's men who "sailed to Ophir and brought back 420 talents of gold, which they delivered to King Solomon." Although this city's exact location still remains a mystery (with conjectures ranging from the Somali coast of Africa to India), its existence and assets have been independently attested. A potsherd from the mid-eighth century B.C. has been unearthed at a port north of Tel Aviv. It carried the clear notation of the contents marked by a local clerk saying, "Ophir gold for Beth-Horon: 30 shekels" (about 340 g., 12 oz.).[14]

One conclusion can be safely made: Solomon's golden temple was no mere invention of exaggerating scribes. It falls into the known patterns of ancient practices of his times.

ISRAEL AND MOAB'S CONFLICT ON STONE!

Some of the objects unearthed by archaeologists give very specific details of biblical events. One example of this is a stone memorial that tells of a conflict between Moab and Israel presented in 2 Kings 3. The Bible notes that Mesha, the king of Moab, and his people rebelled against Israel's rule over them and refused to pay tribute. A battle raged between Moab and the three kings of Israel, Judah and Edom. The

Moabites won the battle and Israel abandoned its rule over them.

In an 1868 excavation a German named Klein found an inscribed stone at Dibon, the land of Moab. Since the stone was owned by Arabs living at Dibon, he returned home to raise money for its purchase. The Arabs, thinking they could get a higher price for it, roasted the stone and then threw cold water over it to break it into pieces. Fortunately, Klein had taken an impression of the intact stone, so it was possible to restore the fragments and translate them after its purchase. It is now at the Louvre in Paris. In an early form of the Phoenician alphabet (an area of present-day Syria), the inscription describes Mesha, king of Moab, with the help of his god Chemosh, had throne off the rule of Israel. King Omri of Israel, Ahab's father, is referred to by name in the inscription along with a number of biblical places. Significantly, it mentions the God of Israel, called "Yahweh."[15]

DANIEL AND BELSHAZZAR

From a host of other discoveries, Daniel's account of the irreverent King Belshazzar stands out. Daniel names Belshazzar as the last king of Babylon. Yet all known Babylonian records listed Nabonidus as the last king. An obvious discrepancy, an error!

Then it was discovered in a Babylonian chronicle that Nabonidus inexplicably removed himself for a ten-year stint in Arabia, leaving the kingdom in the hands of his son Belshazzar. The confusion came because Nabonidus did not abdicate the kingship. He was still called king. Although Belshazzar was not the sole king, Daniel and the Hebrew young men with him considered him as the de facto king. Prior to the study of the Babylonian chronicles, Belshazzar was mentioned only in the biblical record.

The archaeologist R. F. Dougherty concludes after his study of these findings: "Of all non-Babylonian records dealing with the situation at the close of the Neo-Babylonian Empire, [the description of events in] . . . chapter five of the book of Daniel ranks next to cuneiform literature in accuracy."[16]

NEW TESTAMENT VERIFIED

Archaeological research and discovery for the New Testament has been of a different nature than for the Old. It is not so much a matter of digging for buried buildings or inscribed tablets; rather, New Testament archaeology is primarily a matter of written documents. F. F. Bruce comments:

These documents may be *public or private inscriptions* on stone or some equally durable material: they may be papyri recovered from the sand of Egypt recording literary texts or housewives' shopping lists; they may be private notes scratched on fragments of unglazed pottery; they may be legends on coins preserving information about some otherwise forgotten government ruler or getting some point of official propaganda across to the people who used them.

They may also represent a Christian *church's collection of sacred Scriptures,* like the Chester Beatty Biblical Papyri; they may be all that is left of the library of an ancient religious community, like the scrolls from Qumran or the Gnostic texts from Nag Hammadi. But whatever their character, they can be as important and relevant for the study of the New Testament as any cuneiform tablets are for the study of the Old.[17]

The common people wrote letters on papyrus and kept ordinary commercial accounts of life on it. An even cheaper writing material was broken pieces of pottery, called "ostraca." These were used for odd notes. (By the way, if you want your notes kept for a thousand years, put them on ostraca!)

Some pieces discovered in ancient rubbish heaps have shown the connection between the everyday language of the common people and the Greek in which most of the New Testament is written. Comparing these finds helps validate the differences between the Greek of classic literature and that of the New Testament. Through the discoveries of the papyri it is evident the New Testament Greek was very similar to the language of the common people.

In 1931 the discovery of an extraordinary collection of papyrus texts of the Greek Scriptures was made public. They have come to be known as the Chester Beatty Biblical Papyri and are a collection of Greek Scriptures used by some outlying church in Egypt, folded and arranged like a bound book.[18] This collection is composed of eleven fragmentary codices on leaves of papyrus paper, with three of the eleven containing most of

Spiritual truth comes as we look beyond the archaeological finds to God himself.

the New Testament. One contains the four Gospels and the book of Acts. A Pauline codex is the oldest of the eleven, and it was written at the beginning of the third century. It contains nine letters of Paul, the Epistle to the Hebrews and Revelation.

Even in their present mutilated state these papyri bear important testimony to the early textual history of the New Testament. Already referred to in chapter six is John's Gospel dated around A.D. 100 and is the oldest known fragment of any part of the New Testament.

STONE INSCRIPTIONS

Inscriptions on stone have been another source of valuable information. An example of this is an edict of Claudius inscribed on limestone at Delphi in central Greece. Again, F. F. Bruce writes:

> This edict is to be dated [as originating] during the first seven months of A.D. 52, and mentions Gallio as being proconsul of Achaia. We know from other sources that Gallio's proconsulship lasted only for a year, and since proconsuls entered on their term of office on July 1, the inference is that Gallio entered his proconsulship on that date in A.D. 51. But Gallio's proconsulship of Achaia overlapped Paul's year and a half of ministry in Corinth (Acts 18:11-12) so that Claudius' inscription provides us with a fixed point for reconstructing the chronology of Paul's career.[19]

82

Luke, a true historian, has been noted for his accuracy of detail. An example of his precision is his reference in Luke 3:1 to "Lysanias, the tetrarch of Abilene" or ruler of a quarter of a region. This man was one of those in charge at the time when John the Baptist began his ministry A.D. 27. Mention of Lysanias has been regarded as a mistake because the only ruler of that name known from ancient historians was King Lysanias, whom Antony executed at Cleopatra's instigation in 36 B.C., more than fifty years before John the Baptist.

Then a Greek inscription from Abila (eighteen miles westnorthwest of Damascus), from which the territory of Abilene is named, records a dedication to one Nymphaeus "free man of Lysanias, the tetrarch" between A.D. 14 and A.D. 29, around the very time indicated by Luke. Again, accuracy has been supported.[20]

NO PIOUS FORGERY

Archaeology confirms the accounts recorded in the Bible.

• *Coins* have provided some background information for parts of New Testament history. One of the crucial facts to establish the chronology of Paul's career is the date of Felix's replacement by Festus as procurator of Judea (Acts 24:27). A new Judean coinage began in Nero's fifth year, before October of A.D. 59. This may point to the beginning of the new procuratorship.

• *Sacred sites* have been definitely identified and general locations have also been uncovered. General locations have been more easily established than exact spots where some of the great New Testament events transpired.

• *Jerusalem* was destroyed in A.D. 70 and a new pagan city was founded on the site in A.D. 135. This has complicated the identification of places in Jerusalem mentioned in the Gospels and Acts. Some, however, like the temple area and the Pool of Siloam, to which our Lord sent the blind man to wash (John 9:11), have been clearly identified.

Archaeology is a valuable help in understanding the Bible. It yields fascinating information that illuminates what might otherwise be obscured and in some instances confirms what some might otherwise regard as doubtful.

We can agree with Keith N. Schoville who says: "It is important to realize that archaeological excavations have produced ample evidence to prove unequivocally that the Bible is not a pious forgery. Thus far, *no historical statement* in the Bible has proven false on the basis of evidence retrieved through archaeological research."[21]

FOR FURTHER READING

Currid, John D. *Archaeology in the Land of the Bible.* Grand Rapids, Mich.: Baker, 1999.

Free, Joseph P., and Howard Vos. *Archaeology and Bible History.* Grand Rapids, Mich.: Zondervan, 1992.

CHAPTER EIGHT

ARE MIRACLES POSSIBLE?

"Do you really believe that Jonah was swallowed by a whale? And do you seriously think that Christ actually fed five thousand people from five loaves of bread and two fish?" So goes the trend and tone of many modern questioners. Surely, the questions often go, these "miracle" stories in the Bible must be merely quaint ways of conveying spiritual truth and are not meant to be taken literally.

As with all questions we have about God and his existence, the beginning is to discern the root—the underlying issue involved. Otherwise we discuss the twig, not the deeper branch. This is especially true in understanding miracles. It is not the possibility of a particular miracle that is troubling but the whole concept of miracles. To establish the credibility of one miracle would not get to the root. The puzzle is with the *whole possibility of miracles.*

OUR CONCEPT OF GOD

Questions about the credibility of miracles extend also to the validity of predictive prophecy or any supernatural act. All of these questions stem from a concept of God who is conceived of as human, not divine. Once we assume the existence and character of God, miracles are no longer a problem. God is by definition all-powerful. In the absence of such a God, the concept of miracles becomes difficult, if not impossible, to entertain.

This came to me very forcibly one day as I was talking about the deity of Christ with a Japanese professor friend. "I find it very difficult to believe," he said, "that a man could become God." Sensing his problem, I replied, "Yes, Kinichi, so do I, but I can believe that God could become a man." He saw the difference in a flash, and not long afterward he saw the rationale of God in Christ coming to earth, and he became a Christian.

IS GOD BOUND BY NATURAL LAW?

The question, then, reverts to "Does an all-powerful God, who created the universe, exist?" If so, we shall have little difficulty with miracles. If so, he transcends the natural law of which he is the author. Reviewing our fundamental view of God, that he is alive, active, powerful and caring will help our thinking about miracles.

Philosopher David Hume and others have defined a miracle as a violation of natural law. Such a position, however, practically deifies natural law. This capitalizes it in such a way that God becomes the prisoner of natural law and in effect ceases to be God.

In this modern scientific age, it is common to personify science and natural law. This sidesteps the fact that these laws are merely the impersonal results of our observation, sometimes even making natural law the *deity*. The Christian views natural law as behaving in an observable cause-and-effect way, all the time—year after year, century after century. At the same time the Bible does not restrict God's right and power to intervene when and how he chooses. God is outside, over and above natural law, and is not bound by it.

Natural laws do not cause anything in the sense that God causes and creates. These are merely descriptions of what we observe happening.

WHAT IS A MIRACLE?

Miracle is a word used rather loosely today. If a scared student passes an exam, he says, "It was a miracle!" Or if our old, worn-out van makes a successful trip from one city to another, we say, "It's a miracle the thing ran!" We use the term to mean anything that is unusual or unexpected. We do not necessarily mean that the hand of God has been at work.

Miracles, as recorded in the Bible, are acts of God. This is an entirely different sense than we use in common speech. The biblical use is an act of God breaking into, changing or interrupting the ordinary course of things.

• The Bible records various kinds of miracles, and some of them could have a *natural explanation*. For instance, the account in Exodus 14 tells of God parting a lane through the Red Sea to help the Israelites escape slavery in Egypt. Some have conjectured that the sea parted naturally by high winds driving the waters back. Perhaps this might have happened apart from God's intervention, but the miraculous part was the *timing*. The high winds would have had to come just as the Israelites reached the shore as the Egyptians closed in with hot pursuit. Then after every Israelite was safely across and on dry land, the wind would have had to die down and stop the Egyptians from following. The timing is the evidence of the miraculous intervention of God.

• On the other hand, there are many miracles for which *no natural explanation* arises. The resurrection of Lazarus from the dead and the resurrection of Jesus Christ both involve forces unknown to us and outside the realm of so-called natural law. The same is true of the record of Jesus' many healings.

Jesus himself is the one convincing and permanent miracle!

• We might be tempted to explain these in terms of *psychosomatic* response, but the healings of Jesus were clearly outside this category. The healings of leprosy are a case in point. Obviously these did not have a psychosomatic base, arising as the disease does from a bacterial invasion of the body. Lepers who were healed experienced the direct power of God. Also, there are cases of congenital diseases being healed. The man born blind could not possibly be accounted for on a psychosomatic basis. Nor could it have accounted for his receiving his sight (John 9).

• Another notion commonly expressed is that people in ancient times were exceedingly ignorant, gullible and superstitious. No doubt they thought many things were miracles that we now know *were not miracles at all but simply phenomena they did not understand*. Our understanding has expanded exponentially thanks to the benefits of modern science. For example, if we were to fly a modern jet over a primitive tribe today, they would probably fall to the ground in worship of this "silver bird god" of the sky. They would think that the sight they observed was a miraculous phenomenon, a miracle. We would know that the plane is simply a result of the applied principles of aerodynamics, and there is nothing miraculous

87

about it at all.

In the case of the blind man, there was a realistic view of his situation. The people observed that since the beginning of time it had not been known for a man born blind to receive his sight. They weren't dummies! And we have no more natural explanation of Jesus healing him other than was available then. And who today has any more explanation, in a natural sense, of Jesus' resurrection from the dead than was available when it happened? No one! We simply cannot get away from the supernatural aspects of the biblical record.

NO CONFLICT WITH NATURAL LAW

It is important to note, however, that miracles are not in conflict with any natural law. Professor J. N. Hawthorne puts it, "Miracles are *unusual events* caused by God. The laws of nature are generalizations about *ordinary events* caused by him."[1]

There are two views among thinking Christians as to the relationship of miracles to natural law.

• First, miracles employ a "higher" natural law, which at present is unknown to us. It is quite obvious that despite all of the impressive discoveries of modern science, we are still standing on the seashore of an ocean of ignorance. When our knowledge increases sufficiently, this thesis says, we will realize that the things we thought were miracles were merely the working of the higher laws of the universe, of which we were not aware at the time.

A law, in the modern scientific sense, is that which is regular and acts uniformly. To say that a miracle is the result of a higher law, then, we would not admit to any deviation from natural law.

• Second, biblical miracles are an act of creation—a sovereign, transcendent act of God's supernatural power. It would seem that this is the more appropriate view.

> Miracles are not contrary to nature but only contrary to what we know about nature.

BIBLICAL MIRACLES

Biblical miracles were never capricious or fantastic, in contrast to miracle stories in pagan literature and those of other religions. They were not scattered helter-skelter through the record without rhyme or reason. There was always clear order and purpose to them. They cluster

around three periods of biblical history:
- the Exodus,
- the prophets who led Israel and
- the time of Christ and the early church.

In the biblical recordings of miracles each always had one purpose: to confirm faith. They authenticated the message and the messenger, or they demonstrated God's love by relieving suffering.

They were never performed as entertainment, as a magician putting on a show for his patrons.

Miracles were never performed for personal prestige or to gain money or power. Jesus was tempted by the devil in the wilderness to use his miracle power in just this way, but he steadfastly refused. He referred to the centrality of God in the use of any demonstration of miracles (see Luke 4:1-13).

In answer to the direct request of the Jews to tell them plainly if he was the Messiah, Jesus said, "I did tell you, but you do not believe. The miracles I do in my Father's name speak for me" (John 10:25). Again he says that if they had any hesitation in believing his claims, they should believe him "on the evidence of the miracles themselves" (John 14:11).

God used miracles in the fledgling church to confirm their message, which repeatedly centered on the miracle of the resurrection. Note the book of Acts.

89

WHY NOT NOW?

People often say, "If God performed miracles then, why does he not do them now? If I saw a miracle I could believe!" This question was answered by Jesus himself. He told of a rich man who was in the torment of hell, lifted up his eyes and pleaded with Abraham that someone should warn his five brothers lest they too should come into the awful place. He was told that his brothers had the Scriptures. But the rich man protested that if someone should rise from the dead, they would be shaken by the miracle and would turn from their present lifestyle and follow Jesus. The reply given applies as much today as then: "If they do not listen to Moses and the Prophets, they will not be convinced even if someone rises from the dead" (Luke 16:31). It's the same today.

This statement of Jesus can speak to us in midst of the pressure of our contemporary cultural norms. Without our awareness our rationalistic presuppositions rule out the very possibility of miracles. Our postmodernistic thinking tells us miracles are impossible; no amount of evidence would ever persuade us one had taken place. Automatically, an alternate, naturalistic explanation would be advanced.

The biblical miracles are always purposeful. A number of times the people who saw Jesus' power asked for more magic or wizardry. However, he repeatedly asserted that his sole purpose was to teach spiritual truth, to demonstrate his own character and his Father's power. His self-definition was to give us life, abundant life, and to reveal God. "Grace and truth came through Jesus Christ" (John 1:17). Each miracle was toward this end.

RELIABLE RECORDS VERIFY THE MIRACLES

Miracles are not necessary for us today as a basis of faith because we have extraordinary records of superior accuracy to show us God's truth. As Ramm observes, "If miracles are capable of sensory perception, they can be made matters of [written] testimony. If they are adequately investigated, the recorded testimony has the same validity for evidence as the experience of beholding the event."[2]

Every court in the world operates on the basis of reliable testimony by word of mouth or in writing. "If the raising of Lazarus was actually witnessed by John and recorded truthfully by him when still in soundness of faculties and memory, for purposes of evidence it is the same as if we were there and saw it."[3] Ramm then lists reasons we may know that the miracles have adequate and reliable testimony. To summarize:

• First, Jesus' miracles were *done in public*. They were not performed in secret before only one or two people, who then announced them to the world. There was every opportunity to investigate the miracles on the spot. It is very impressive that the opponents of Jesus *never denied* the fact of the miracles he performed. They either attributed them to the power of Satan or else tried to suppress the evidence, as with the raising of Lazarus from the dead. They said, in effect, "Let's kill him before the people realize what is happening and the whole world goes after him!"

• Second, Jesus' miracles were *done before unbelievers*. By contrast, miracles claimed by cults and offbeat groups never seem to happen when the skeptic is present to observe. This was not so with Jesus.

• Third, Jesus' miracles were *carried out through three years of ministry, covering a variety of powers*. He displayed power over nature, as when he turned the water to wine. He had power over disease, as when he healed the lepers and the blind. He had power over demons, as was shown by his casting them out. He had supernatural knowledge, as in his knowing that Nathanael was under a fig tree. He demonstrated his power to create when he fed five thousand people from a few loaves and fish. He had power over natural forces as when he calmed the wind and the waves of a strong storm. And finally, he exhibited power over death itself in the raising of Lazarus and others from the dead.

• Fourth, the *testimony of the cured* is undeniable. As noted earlier, we have it from those, like Lazarus, whose healings could not have been psychosomatic or a result of inaccurate diagnosis.

• Fifth, compared to non-Christian religions, these New Testament accounts of Jesus of Nazareth are *extraordinarily unique,* in an entirely different category, with an entirely different purpose. They are but a part of an entire, authentic message: his birth, his message of forgiveness, his death and resurrection.

Miracles are usually believed in other religions because the religion is already believed, but in the biblical religion, miracles are part of the means of establishing the true religion. This distinction is of immense importance. Israel was brought into existence by a series of miracles, the first five books of the Old Testament were surrounded by supernatural wonders. Many of the prophets were identified as God's spokesmen by their power to perform miracles. Jesus came not only preaching but performing miracles, and the apostles from time to time worked wonders. It was the miracle authenticating the religion at every point.[4]

91

As C. S. Lewis wrote, "All the essentials of Hinduism would, I think, remain unimpaired if you subtracted the miraculous, and the same is almost true of Islam, but you cannot do that with Christianity. It is precisely the story of a great miracle. *A naturalistic Christianity would leave out all that is specifically Christian.*"[5]

PAGAN MIRACLES

Miracles recorded outside the Bible differ in order, dignity and motive as those in Scripture. But what is more important, the amazing, solid authentication contained in biblical miracles we've seen in chapter six is missing. Similar investigations into both secular and pagan records of miracles shows the totality of the message is missing. The more we integrate these facts into our thinking, the more accurate will be our judgment of all truth claims.

Using the same standards for judging the alleged miracles and healings we hear in our time aids our thinking. The consistency and authentication of biblical miracles can become the standard by which we judge all other so-called miracles and alleged healings of our time. You will see they do not stand the full weight of investigation. A summary exposure will show they are not equal to biblical miracles. To find some miracles are counterfeit is no proof that all are spurious, any more than the discovery of some counterfeit currency would prove all currency spurious. It helps to compare the broad picture of each one examined.

EXAGGERATED REPORTING

Some attempts have been made to explain away miracles on the basis of exaggerated reporting, especially by Jesus' followers. In general, we could say people are notoriously inaccurate in reporting events and impressions. Play the simple party game of "Rumor" in which a secret is whispered from person to person around a room and see the details change through transmission. In the light of this tendency, some say it is obvious that the reliability of any human being as an observer may be easily discounted. On this basis, we can discount the gospel accounts of miracles as the mistaken observations of inaccurate and imaginative observers.

Despite this tendency, our law courts have not ceased functioning, and eyewitnesses are still considered able to provide highly useful information. And though there may be some question about an automobile accident, details of the eyewitnesses can give the time, speed of the cars, location and so forth. The accident cannot be said not to have happened because of discrepancies in witnesses' stories. As Ramm observes, the smashed cars and the injured people are irrefutable evidence on which all agreed.[6]

Of course, we see there may be limitations to the arguments given such as the reliability of the witnesses. All considerations would be given to help us see that some of the arguments when pressed to their outer limits refute the very assertions they set out to make. For instance, those

Miracles do not appear on the pages of Scripture vagrantly. They appear when God is speaking to his people through accredited messengers.

conducting the reliability or unreliability of a human witness is assuming their own reliability. Put another way, if one person says another's testimony is unreliable, there is the equal possibility that person's own testimony is unreliable.

BELIEVERS CAN'T BE OBJECTIVE

One questionable idea, sometimes advanced, is that the miracle stories must be discarded because they are told by believing disciples and are therefore not objective. But the disciples were the ones on the scene who saw the miracles. The fact that they were disciples is neither here nor there. The question is, Did they tell the *truth?* As we have seen, eyewitness testimony is the best we can get, and most of the disciples faced the specter of death as the test of their veracity.

In our courts of law, we would not say that in order to guarantee objectivity on the part of witnesses, we will only listen to those not at the scene of an accident and had nothing to do with it. Nor would we say we would not take testimony from eyewitnesses or victims, claiming they would be prejudiced. The crucial question in each case is truthfulness, not proximity or relationship to the events.

THE QUESTION IS PHILOSOPHICAL

The fundamental question of whether miracles are possible is not scientific, but philosophical. Science can only say miracles do not occur in the ordinary course of nature. *Science cannot forbid miracles because natural laws do not cause and therefore cannot forbid anything.* Natural laws, as we see them, are merely descriptions of what happens.

The Christian also embraces the concept of natural law. "It is essential to the theistic doctrine of miracles that nature be uniform [predictable] in her daily routine. If nature were utterly spontaneous [unpredictable], miracles would be as impossible to detect as it would be to establish a natural law."[7]

This difference between the Christian and the scientist is philosophical since each has distinctive presuppositions, the base of all our opinions. The possibility of seeing something as a miracle, then, depends on our presuppositions, our point of view or our worldview.

What then, is the presupposition of the Christian? *God exists, has originated natural law, can make or break it, can intervene or not.* The supernatural, personal God is at the base of all phenomena, natural and spiritual. G. K. Chesterton said, "A miracle is startling; but it is simple. It is simple because it is a miracle. It is power coming directly from God instead of indirectly through nature or human wills."[8]

What, then, is the presupposition of the agnostic or atheistic scientist? *God does not, cannot exist.* Scientists (unless they are Christian) generally make all judgments and opinions based on naturalistic, materialistic observations, believing there is no other option. From this presupposition the supernatural does not intrude and indeed would not be considered. The scientist, like anyone else, can only ask, "Are the records of miracles historically reliable?" He or she will go no further.

As a summary of thoughts on miracles, we have seen the miracles in the Bible as an inherent part of God's communication to us—not a mere appendage of little significance. It also takes us back again to the ultimate question, does God exist? Settle that question and miracles cease to be a problem. The very uniformity against which a miracle stands in stark contrast depends on an omnipotent Author of natural law, who is also capable of transcending it to accomplish his sovereign ends.

FOR FURTHER READING

Connelly, Doug. *Miracles.* Downers Grove, Ill.: InterVarsity Press, 1998.

Fischer, Robert B. *God Did It, But How? Relationships Between the Bible and Science.* 2nd ed. Ipswich, Mass.: American Scientific Affiliation, 1997.

Lewis, C. S. *Miracles.* New York: Simon & Schuster, 1996.

CHAPTER NINE

DO SCIENCE & SCRIPTURE AGREE?

If ever there was a question that generated more heat than light, it is this one: Do science and Scripture agree? No doubt there is conflict. On one hand there are Christians who claim the Bible says things it really does not say. On the other hand, there are scientists who claim their philosophic interpretations are the same as scientific fact (called scientism). When these interpretations don't seem to square with the Bible, again there is a problem.

95

To the question "Have some scientists and Christians disagreed?" the answer would have to be a resounding yes! We need only recall the Pope's persecution of Galileo for claiming the earth revolved around the sun, the Scopes trial of 1925 regarding the teaching creation or evolution in the schools, or the slavery controversy two centuries ago between Wilberforce and Huxley to know this is the case.

WELL-MEANING CHRISTIANS

Part of the problem, as I have indicated, stems from some well-meaning but misguided Christians who make the Bible say what it does not say. One classic and harmful example is the Bible chronology calculated by Bishop James Ussher (1581-1656), a contemporary of Shakespeare. He worked out a series of dates from the genealogies in the Bible and concluded that the world was created in 4004 B.C.

It is thought by many skeptics, including the famous Lord Bertrand Russell, that all Christians actually believe creation occurred in 4004 B.C. Some time ago I was visiting a student at a Midwestern state university campus. He picked up a true-false exam from his course on Western civilization. One question read, "According to the Bible, the world was created in 4004 B.C."

"I suppose your instructor wants you to mark this question true," I said.

"That's right," the student replied.

"Interesting," I mused. Pulling an Oxford edition of the Bible from my pocket, I said, "I wonder if you could show me where the Bible says that."

The student was puzzled that he couldn't find the date on the first page of Genesis. Trying to be helpful, a Christian student who was with me volunteered, "It's on page 3."

It was news to both of them that Bishop Ussher's dates, which appear in some English Bibles, are not part of the original text.

On the other hand, some scientists have been known to make statements beyond the facts. These statements are philosophic interpretations of data, which do not carry the same weight of authority as hard data. Unfortunately, the facts and the interpretations are seldom distinguished in the minds of listeners.

WHEN A SCIENTIST SPEAKS

A scientist speaking on any subject is likely to believed. He may be speaking outside his field, but the same respect given to his statements within his field are almost unconsciously transferred to everything he says. Who can argue with such erudition? For instance, the late Carl Sagan, well-known author and former professor of astronomy at Cornell University, illustrates this crossover from science to "scientism," a purely personal philosophical opinion. *U.S. News and World Report* interviewed him on the subject of science and religion! Science is his field; religion certainly is not! However, he made bold religious pronouncements: "The cosmos is all that is or ever was or ever will be"; "Whatever significance we humans have is that which we make ourselves"; and "If we must worship a power greater than ourselves, does it not make sense to worship the sun and the stars?" But why would we worship nature if it is, as he states, "the result of blind chance and part of a pointless process"?[1]

FAITH IS SUSPECT

Another area in which conflict has arisen is on the question of whether those things that cannot be verified by the scientific method are valid and real. Some people consciously, and others unconsciously, assume that if a statement cannot be proved in a laboratory by the methods of natural science, it is untrustworthy and cannot be accepted as reliable. The findings of science are considered to be objective and therefore real; statements that must be accepted by faith are looked on as suspect.

E. O. Wilson, a widely respected biologist, illustrates this position in his book *On Human Nature*. He states, "The final decisive edge enjoyed by scientific naturalism will come from its capacity to explain traditional religion, its chief competitor, as a wholly material phenomenon."[2]

But there are ways and means other than the laboratory to acquire real and genuine knowledge. Consider the process of falling in love. This surely is not done in a laboratory with a battery of instruments, but anyone who has ever experienced it would be the last to admit their knowledge of love is uncertain or unreal. Other presuppositions of science include the existence of truth, laws of logic, the adequacy of language and numbers. The simple fact is that true, rationally justified beliefs exist in a host of fields outside of science.[3] The scientific method is valid only for those realities that are measurable in physical terms.

God is a different kind of reality from the world of nature that science examines. God does not await someone's empirical investigation; he is a spiritual being who exists outside of time and space. Yet he is a *personal being* who has revealed himself in history and can be known in personal presence.

THE SCIENTIST USES FAITH

Faith is no detriment to the apprehension of reality. In fact, science itself rests on presuppositions that must be accepted by faith before research is possible.

The universe is orderly. It operates according to a pattern, and therefore can be examined and its behavior can be predicted. This would include the uniformity of our world and it will continue as it is presently. For example, apples will always fall down, not up!

Objective truth exists and is knowable. If the object of the scientist's study were solely materialistic and naturalistic, all of the effort would be confined to these naturalistic phenomena. One might say that the scientist's truth would not extend beyond these measurable areas. The underlying presupposition is that things which cannot be examined under a microscope or with a telescope undoubtedly do not exist.

The reliability of the sense perceptions. This is another nonphysical presupposition that must be accepted by faith. One must believe that our senses are trustworthy enough to get a true picture of the universe and enable us to understand its orderliness.

The repeatability of a laboratory experiment. When a work by a scientist gets published and is repeated by another scientist, the results ought to be the same. Put hydrogen and oxygen together in the proper proportions, you will get water . . . given the same conditions. As we discussed earlier, however, many things, such as history, are nonrepeatable in a laboratory.

It should be observed here that the scientific method, as we know it today, began in the sixteenth century among people who were Christians. They broke with the Greek polytheistic concepts that viewed the universe as capricious and irregular and therefore not capable of systematic study. They then reasoned that the universe must be orderly and worthy of investigation because it was the work of an intelligent Creator. In pursuing scientific research they were convinced that they were thinking God's thoughts after him.

Many recognize that science is incapable of making *value judgments* about the things it measures. Many people on the frontiers of science are realizing that there is nothing inherent in science to guide them in the *application* of the discoveries they make. There is nothing in science itself that will determine whether nuclear energy will be used to destroy cities or cancer; this is a judgment outside the scientific method's scope.

Science can tell us how something works but not why it works in a particular way. Whether there is any purpose in the universe can never be answered by science. As one writer put it, science can give us the "'know-how,' but it cannot give us the 'know-why.'"[4] We are dependent on revelation for many kinds of information, the absence of which leaves us with a quite incomplete picture.

Both Sides Have Presuppositions

All people have a worldview, a set of presuppositions, through which we filter all other information. Christians believe science is one avenue for the discovery of Truth—with a capital T. Also, God exists, is active in his creation and is our seminal frame of reference. A Christian sees nothing incompatible between reason or intelligence and faith in a supernatural God. Those Christians who are scientists do not consider themselves intellectual schizophrenics but rather view themselves as following in the footsteps of the Christian founders of modern science.

To illustrate this, William Paley in the eighteenth century couched this view for us:

> Suppose I had found a *watch* upon the ground, and it should be inquired how the watch happened to be in that place. I should hardly think the answer would be … the watch must have always been there. Of course, the watch must have had a maker, that existed before, an artificer who formed it; . . . someone who comprehended its construction and designed its use.[5]

This expresses the Christian's presupposition. God, the Creator, existed *before* the world was made, and he was and is "an artificer" who formed it and designed it. Science, along with any other data, is seen through this God-focused filter.

The entire revelation of the Bible is built on this premise; God has revealed himself, and he is the Creator. Jesus said, "You will know the truth and the truth will set you free" (John 8:32). It is possible to differentiate between truth and error.

The agnostic (or atheist) scientist, on the other hand, also has presuppositions quite different than the Christian's. Despite the most detailed, complex discoveries, Darwin's basic evolutionary mechanism strongly persists and is even fought for. Random variation (mutation) and natural selection are clung to. Atheist Richard Dawkins claims that everything, including our minds, can be "reduced" to its material base. He says, "We are survival machines—robot vehicles blindly programmed to preserve the selfish molecules (of DNA which survived) known as genes." Later he seemed to be having second thoughts, saying, "The objects and phenomena that a physics book describes are *simpler* than a single cell in the body of its author."[6]

The impact of Paley's watchmaker analogy still persists and provokes not a little attention with its inarguable logic. Taking up the argument, Dawkins authored the book *The Blind Watchmaker*. To disparage Paley's "artificer" idea and explain the existence of the watch, he champions natural selection: "It has no mind and no mind's eye. It does not plan for the future. It has no vision, no foresight, no sight at all. If it can be said to play the role of watchmaker in nature, it is the *blind* watchmaker!"[7]

THE BLACK BOX OPENED

The continuing discussions using the watchmaker analogy has brought forth the inscrutability and even wonder regarding the details of natural life. Michael Behe, a molecular biologist, in his book *Darwin's Black Box* opens up several processes vital to life, such as blood clotting and vision. Whereas Darwin could conceive of gradual changes that explain visible modification, he knew virtually nothing of the complexity of processes at a molecular level.

One sample of Behe's illustrations explains how the retina of the eye accommodates and rearranges itself when light enters it. When light first strikes the retina a photon interacts with a molecule called 11-cis retinal, rearranging it to be a trans-retinal within picoseconds. (A picosecond is about the time it takes light to travel the breadth of a single human hair.)[8] A cascade of chemical reactions continues to occur, each step necessary for the next, all necessary for us to see. No explanation excepting intelligent design accounts for all these reactions. Leave out even one, and we simply won't be able to see. How could this order of reactions happen through gradualism if they are *all* necessary for vision? Biochemistry here points us *toward* belief in a designer.

Other similar illustrations could be cited. The meticulous function of the estimated sixty to eighty thousand genes of the human genome screams loudly of an intelligent programmer. Our DNA, proteins and RNA are information banks holding in detail our personal characteristics: our height, hair, color of eyes, fingerprint, brain cells, and so on. Each human being, except for identical twins, holds his or her own profile. Made up of spiral chemical ladders, they are so intricate and unique that Behe concludes that a Designer is firmly indicated. His memorable term for the human genome is *irreducible complexity; nothing can be left out.*[9]

The idea of the "irreducibility" of a single molecule is illustrated by Behe in the construction of a simple mousetrap. The piece of wood, the spring, the lever for the cheese all must be there. Take out one part and you will not catch a mouse. Similarly, a molecule is irreducibly complex, albeit a thousand times more complex than a mousetrap.

Molecular mechanisms are as obviously designed as a spaceship or a computer. You cannot explain the origin of any biological capability (like vision) unless you can explain the molecular mechanisms that make it work.[10]

Examples of "irreducible complexity"

• DNA—molecules holding the blueprints for the construction of life.

• RNA—molecules carrying the blueprints from the DNA to specific proteins.

• Proteins—molecules that follow portions of the blueprints in building and repairing life molecules.

Could such incredible complexity come together by the chance appearance of these molecules at the same time and place? It is beyond the realm of statistical possibility. It screams "intelligent design." Nonetheless, Darwinian evolutionary science continues to deny even the possibility of a Designer to explain these intricate, otherwise unexplainable features of nature.

CHECK OUT THE MEANING OF *EVOLUTION*

Whenever the term *evolution* is used, it helps to understand the intended meaning. Also, find out what others mean when they use the word.

The process itself we may call *evolutionism.* Those who hold this worldview believe that the universe has been evolving forever exclusively on the basis of natural processes, mutation and natural selection. Relying on chance, it is the "survival of the fittest" (a *process* which demonstrably can be seen in two categories).

• First is *microevolution,* which describes a continued process of change or development but only *within a species.* Swedish naturalist Carolus Linnaeus explained that a species is one of seven classifications of all living plants and animals. The groups are: (1) kingdom, (2) phylum, (3) class, (4) order, (5) family, (6) genus and (7) species. The kingdom is the largest group, and the species is the smallest. Members of a species have a high degree of similarity among themselves and generally interbreed only with themselves. G. A. Kerkut, an evolutionist, described microevolution as "many living animals observed over the course of time which undergo change so that new [varieties] are formed."[11] Note the emphasis for this is *within a species.*

In microevolution the changes may be chromosome changes,

gene mutations or hybridization to produce new varieties. These changes take place always within an individual species. As has been said, "A horse is still a horse." Or, *"No protozoa to a man."*

To illustrate, if a mutation takes place within the genes of the earthworm, providing it with increased dexterity against predatory blackbirds, the carriers of this mutation will fare better in the earthworm's struggle for survival. This mutation will improve the worm—but strictly as a worm. This is microevolution within a single species.

Microevolution allows for new variations to arise but not the development of one species to a higher classification. The evidence is substantial and many contemporary Christian scholars agree that this kind of microevolution takes place.[12]

• The second view is *macroevolution,* also called megaevolution, which requires the transfer of genetic information to a higher, more complex classification, the boundaries, as this view sees it, being crossed by mutation and natural selection.

A. E. Wilder-Smith, a professor of pharmacology, points out that these factors along with chance "cannot provide the information necessary to build *legs onto a fish,* thus permitting it to leave the water and to walk on land. Paleontology, for example, knows of no missing links (transitional forms) between whales and land mammals that have ever been established. Intermediate links of this sort would probably have been incapable of living. For over 120 years geology has been searching for these links in vain."[13] Actually, it is erroneous to speak of *the* missing link. There are thousands of missing links!

HOW DOES GOD FIT IN?

For some, God is considered only whenever life and existence have no other explanation. Unbelieving scientists tend to look on this view as evidence that the gaps are narrowing between theism and science. "Give us enough time," they might say, "and humans will be able to explain how everything in the universe works."

This point of view would not square with the description of the Creator we saw in chapter two. God who made this world is not only its Creator but also its sustainer. "He is before all things, and in him all things hold together" (Colossians 1:17). The universe would fall apart without the *sustaining power* of the Creator. A scientific mechanism showing how the universe is sustained *is not the same* as sustaining it. This view of an active Creator involved in the creation continually is called *theism.*

Suppose God would take his sustaining power from the universe and "let the clock run down." Let's give that a thought! As Phillip Johnson says, this would mean God made the laws, set up the physical structures and then retired. This view is called *deism*.

A common question asked is, "Could God have made the world but used the process of evolution?" One necessary question in response would be, What is meant by *evolution?* By its common definition, *evolution* is a mindless, unguided, purposeless and solely material process.

God does not fit into this definition! The concept of God's initial act followed by the gradual unfolding of creation is referred to as *gradualism,* a theory that, according to Johnson, is not supported by the fossil record: "If God did [create the universe using evolution], He also chose not to leave the evidence of it lying around."[14] God would have no place in this process. Nor does the biblical account of a personal God fit this image.

Theism, on the other hand, sees God as both Creator and actively involved, in a supervisory role, in the world and with the people he made.[15] He is invisible but nonetheless real and involved with this world.

Advances made recently in the fields of genetic engineering, microbiology, astrophysics, etc., are evoking undreamed of possibilities and possibly new questions for science. Three insistent thoughts center on the key word *information:*

- Life consists of not only *matter* (chemicals) but *information.*
- Where (or from whom) did the *information* originate?
- Complex, specified *information* comes from an intelligent mind.

The advances in science give credence to the fact that life did not come by blind chance but by an intelligent mind, the result of superior knowledge. Recent discoveries would argue for theism rather than its opposite. And, of course, where did the original elements of life come from? Could they have merely evolved? Now called "the soup theory," the theory that life began in a primordial sauce of chemicals is being questioned. The most logical explanation is that God created those elements.

SCIENCE AND SCRIPTURE MOVING CLOSER?

Some new developments in science have supported the Christian view of a Creator God in surprising ways. This does not mean the scientists have all become theists, but there are a number of areas where there is agreement on both biblical and scientific issues.

• *The universe had a beginning.* In April 1992 news media and scientists from around the globe proclaimed a great breakthrough. The Cosmic Background Explorer (CBOE) satellite found a "stunning confirmation of *the hot big bang* creation event."

"It's the most exciting thing that's happened in my lifetime," stated Carlos Frank of Durham University in Britain.

"It is the discovery of the century, if not of all time," famed British physicist Stephen Hawking affirmed.

"It's like looking at God. We have found the evidence for the birth of the universe," declared George Smoot of the University of California.

Biblical Statements of Cosmological Significance

• God existed "before the universe" yet can be in it. (Colossians 1:16-17)

• Time had a beginning. God precedes time. (2 Timothy 1:9)

• Jesus Christ created the universe. He has no beginning and was not created. (John 1:3)

• God created the universe from what our five senses cannot detect. (Hebrews 11—13)

• Jesus evidenced his extradimensionality after his resurrection. He passed through walls. (John 20:26-28)

• God is very near, yet we cannot see him. He is extradimensional. (Deuteronomy 30:11-14)

• God designed the universe in a way to support human beings. (Nehemiah 9:6)

These reactions refer, of course, to the discovery of the big bang, the beginning of the universe. Basically, the hot big bang model says the entire physical universe—all matter and energy and even the four dimensions of space and time—burst forth from a state of infinite or

104

near infinite density, temperature and pressure. The universe expanded from a volume very much smaller than the period at the end of this sentence, and now continues to expand.[16]

• *Time had a beginning.* God exists outside of our time as we know it. Even Stephen Hawking said, "Time itself must have a beginning." The early chapters of Genesis tell the story of a God who existed before and apart from the time and universe he created. He is not subject to length, width, height and time. He is the one who brought them into existence. For us, by contrast, time moves only forward!

• *God caused effects even before time.* "In the beginning God created the heavens and the earth" (Genesis 1:1). Then, "For by him were all things created: things in heaven and on earth, visible and invisible. . . . He is before all things, and in him all things hold together" (Colossians 1:16-17). He was existing long before he uttered the words, "Let there be light." We are finite, with a beginning and an end. He is infinite, with no beginning and no end.

• *Fine tuning of the cosmic constants.* The fixed cosmic laws of both our solar system and the entire universe make it possible for life to exist on our planet. These are so precise that if any one of them would vary the most minute fraction, we could not exist. Hugh Ross cited twenty-five of these that affect the earth's temperature, our seasons, our entire atmosphere. If these were adjusted just a hair, sometimes by as little as a millionth of a percent, no life would be possible.[17]

A few of these cosmic constants will be real to us: the strength of gravity, the axial tilt, the oxygen to nitrogen ratio in the atmosphere, the ozone level, seismic activity, carbon dioxide and water vapor levels, the speed of the stars flying apart from one another, the expansion of the universe, the velocity of light, the entropy level of the universe, the force of electricity and the mass of the proton. The existence of these is testimony to the unlikelihood that chance kept these constant.

HUMANITY'S ORIGIN

When we view the evolution and the origins of human beings, the Bible gives two nonnegotiables:

• God supernaturally and deliberately created the heavens and the earth (Genesis 1:1).

• God supernaturally and deliberately created the first man and the first woman (Genesis 1:27).

We do not shrink from these two limits. The Genesis account tells us God made Adam and then made Eve from Adam's side, both "made in God's image." When God breathed into Adam the breath of life, that set him apart from anything else God had made. This was a first! It also rules out the possibility suggested by some that people evolved from any animal ancestor.

It is helpful to read the New Testament references that confirm Adam and Eve as historic (Romans 5:12, 14; 1 Corinthians 15:22, 45; 2 Corinthians 11:3; 1 Timothy 2:13-14; Jude 11). A careful understanding of these passages leaves no room for the possibility that the Genesis story is an allegory.

Francis Schaeffer states: "God gave us religious truths in a book of history and a book that touches on the cosmos as well. What sense does it make for God to give us true religious truths and at the same time place them in a book that is wrong when it touches history and the cosmos?"[18]

WHAT ABOUT THE AGE OF THE EARTH?

From the biblical record some Christians assume the earth must have been created not too many thousands of years before the birth of Christ. Yet they believe from science that the earth must be millions or billions of years old and feel squeamish about it. The question is, Can we date the earth from the biblical records?

Let's look at the use of the Hebrew word for *day.* Can it mean periods of time rather than a single twenty-four hour day? In Genesis 1:31 the word is used to describe the completion of the sixth day, during which God created Adam and Eve.

Genesis 2:15-25 describes God's creative activity on that "day." It also describes Adam's activity: naming *all* the animals, falling into a deep sleep, the creation of Eve—all on the sixth day! It seems that even with the most literal interpretation of this day, the sixth day was a longer period of time.

The use of the same word in other passages shows the Lord's concept of day is not so confined. For instance, "A thousand years in your sight are like a day that has just gone by" (Psalm 90:4) and "With the Lord a day is like a thousand years" (2 Peter 3:8). Geologist Davis Young notes that "the language of Genesis 1 (for example, the development of vegetation on day three) strongly implies the processes of natural growth and development, initiated by the decree of God's word ('Let the land produce vegetation')."

It should be noted that some highly intelligent evangelical scholars interpret the Genesis account as describing twenty-four-hour days, with God creating a "grown-up" universe, and we need to consider their arguments. However, Young speaks to this: "The Christian geologist need not assume that all geological features were created with an appearance of age. He may assume that rocks, mountains, and other geological features of the six days of creation were formed through processes analogous with those of the present. And he has the right to use evidence contained in those rocks to reconstruct the past by analogy with the present. This also helps us avoid the problem of why God should have created a rock deposit that looked as if it had been formed by glacial action but really had not."[19]

In summary, Kantzer states, "As biblical students, therefore, we must remain agnostic about the age of the earth. We have no biblical warrant for ruling out the validity of the commonly accepted geological timetable. Let scientists battle it out on the basis of the scientific evidence, but we should not bolster weak scientific positions with misinterpretations of the Bible conjured up for that purpose. God rarely sees fit merely to gratify our curiosity."[20] In matters where God chooses to be silent, we should likewise choose to remain silent.

A Constantly Moving Train

Scientific theory attempts to describe the most probable explanation based on the data available. There are no absolutes in it. Science is a train that is constantly moving. Yesterday's generalization is today's discarded hypothesis. This is one reason for being somewhat tentative about accepting any form of evolutionary theory as the final explanation of biology. It is also why it has become dangerous to try to prove the Bible by science. If the Bible becomes wedded to today's scientific theories, what will happen to it when science, ten years from now, has shifted?

Theologian W. A. Criswell cites: "In 1861 . . . the French Academy of Science published a little brochure in which they stated fifty-one scientific facts that controverted the Word of God. Today there is not a scientist in the world who believes a single one of those fifty-one so-called scientific facts that in 1861 were published as controverting the Word of God. Not a one!"[21]

Thoughtful scientists concede that evolution is not an open-and-shut case, but they feel the theory must be accepted despite some seeming contradictions and unexplained factors.

G. A. Kerkut, an evolutionist, writes of his perspective that theology students at Cambridge, in a former century, had placidly accepted dogma and teachings they did not personally investigate. Kerkut then observes that some present-day students have done like-wise. He writes:

> For some years now I have tutored undergraduates on various aspects of biology. It is quite common, during the course of conversation, to ask the student if he knows the evidence for evolution. This usually evokes a faintly superior smile. . . . "Well, sir, there is the evidence from paleontology, comparative anatomy, embryology, systematic and geographical distributions," the student would say in a nursery-rhyme jargon. . . .
>
> "Do you think that the evolutionary theory is the best explanation yet advanced to explain animal inter-relationships?" I would ask.
>
> "Why, of course, sir," would be the reply. "There is nothing else, except for the religious explanation held by some fundamentalist Christians, and I gather, sir, that these views are no longer held by the more up-to-date churchmen."
>
> "So you believe in evolution because there is no other theory?"
>
> "Oh, no, sir, I believe in it because of the evidence I just mentioned."
>
> "Have you read any book on the evidence for evolution?" I would ask.
>
> "Yes, sir." And here he would mention the names of authors of a popular school textbook. "And of course, sir, there is that book by Darwin, *The Origin of Species.*"
>
> "Have you read this book?" I would ask.
>
> "Well, not all through, sir."
>
> "The first fifty pages?"
>
> "Yes, sir, about that much; maybe a bit less."
>
> "I see. And that has given you your firm under-standing of evolution?"
>
> "Yes, sir."
>
> "Well, now, if you really understand an argument you will be able to indicate to me not only the points in favor of the argument, but also the most telling points against it."
>
> "I suppose so, sir."

Here the conversation would take on a more strained atmosphere. The student would look at me as if I were playing a very unfair game. He would take it rather badly when I suggest that he was not being very scientific in his outlook if he swallowed the latest scientific dogma and, when questioned, just repeated parrot-fashion the views of the current Archbishop Evolution. In fact he would be behaving like certain of those religious students he affected to despise. He would be taking on faith what he could not intellectually understand and, when questioned, would appeal to authority of a "good book," which in this case was *The Origin of Species.* (It is interesting to note that many of these widely quoted books are read by title only. Three of such that come to mind are the Bible, *The Origin of Species,* and *Das Kapital.*)

I would suggest that the student should go away and read the evidence for and against evolution and present it as an essay. A week would pass and the same student would appear armed with an essay on the evidence for evolution. The essay would usually be well done, since the student might have realized that I should be rough to convince. When the essay had been read and the question concerning the evidence against evolution came up, the student would give a rather pained smile. "Well, sir, I looked up various books but could not find anything in the scientific books against evolution. I did not think you would want a religious argument."

"No, you were quite correct. I want a scientific argument against evolution."

"Well, sir there does not seem to be one, and that in itself is a piece of evidence in favor of the evolutionary theory."

I would then indicate to him that the theory of evolution was of considerable antiquity, and would mention that he might have looked at the book by Radi, *The History of Biological Theories.* Having made sure the student had noted the book down for future reference I would proceed as follows:

"Before one can decide that the theory of evolution

is the best explanation of the present-day range of forms of living material, one should examine all the implications that such a theory may hold. Too often the theory is applied to, say, the development of the horse, and then, because it is held to be applicable there, it is extended to the rest of the animal kingdom with little or no further evidence.

"There are, however, seven basic assumptions that are often not mentioned during discussions of evolution. Many evolutionists ignore the first six assumptions and consider only the seventh.

"The first assumption is that nonliving things gave rise to living material, i.e., that spontaneous generation occurred.

"The second assumption is that spontaneous generation occurred only once.

"The third . . . is that viruses, bacteria, plants, and animals are all interrelated.

"The fourth . . . is that the protozoa gave rise to the metazoa.

"The fifth . . . is that the various invertebrate phyla are interrelated.

"The sixth . . . is that the invertebrates gave rise to the vertebrates.

"The seventh . . . is that the vertebrates and fish gave rise to the amphibia, the amphibia to the reptiles, and the reptiles to the birds and mammals. Sometimes this is expressed in other words, i.e., that the modem amphibia and reptiles had a common ancestral stock and so on.

"For the initial purposes of a discussion on evolution I shall consider that the supporters of the theory of evolution hold that all these seven assumptions are valid, and that these assumptions form the general theory of evolution.

"The first point that I should like to make is that the seven assumptions by their nature are not capable of experimental verification. They assume that a certain series of events has occurred in the past. Thus, though it may be possible to mimic some of these events under present-day conditions, this does not mean that these events must therefore have taken place in the past. All that it shows is that it is possible for such a change to take place. Thus, to change a present-day reptile into a mammal, though of great interest, would not show the way in which the mammals did arise. Unfortunately, we cannot bring about even this change; instead we have to depend upon limited circumstantial evidence for our assumptions."[22]

KEEPING THE FACTS STRAIGHT

To sum up the issue of evolution, there can be two extremes. First is the assumption that evolution has been proven without doubt and that anyone with a brain must accept it. The second is the notion that evolution is "only a theory," with little evidence for it. The so-called conflicts of science and the Bible are often conflicts between interpretations of the facts and reality.

As J. P. Moreland says, "The presupposition one brings to the facts, rather than the facts themselves, determines one's conclusion. For instance, one might be told that his wife was seen riding around town with another man. Knowing his wife, he draws a different conclusion from this fact than does the town gossip. The different conclusions result, not from different facts, but from different presuppositions brought to the fact."[23]

In everything we read and we hear let's ask, "What is this person's presupposition?" so that we may interpret conclusions in this light. There is generally no such thing as total objectivity.

Many have found that God can act in miraculous ways and in the past he often chose to. The Bible discloses he was involved in his original creation and continues in a wise and purposeful relationship with it. While there are problems for which there is as yet no clear explanation, science and Scripture show some signs of becoming strong allies.

FOR FURTHER READING

Dembski, William A., ed. *Mere Creation: Science, Faith & Intelligent Design.* Downers Grove, Ill.: InterVarsity Press, 1998.

Ratzsch, Del. *Science & Its Limits.* Downers Grove, Ill.: InterVarsity Press, 2000.

111

CHAPTER TEN

WHY DOES GOD ALLOW SUFFERING & EVIL?

The question as to why God allows suffering and evil is one of the most pressing of our time. More pressing than the question of miracles, or science and the Bible, is the poignant problem of why innocent people suffer, why babies are born blind or why a promising life is snuffed out as it is on the rise. Why are there wars in which thousands of innocent people are killed, children are burned beyond recognition and many are maimed for life?

The classic summary pinpoints two sides to this dilemma:

• God is *all-powerful* but *not* all-good and therefore doesn't want to stop evil.

• God is *all-good* but *unable* to stop evil; therefore he is not all-powerful.

The general tendency is to blame God for evil and suffering and to pass on all responsibility for it to him.

NO EASY ANSWERS

This profound question is not one to be treated lightly or in a dogmatic fashion. Let's go back and recall what happened when God created Adam and Eve; he created them *perfect*. They were not created evil.

Adam and Eve did, however, as human beings have ability to obey or disobey God. Had they obeyed God, there would never have been a problem. They would have lived an unending life of blissful fellowship with God and enjoyment of him and his creation. This is what God intended for them when he created them. In fact, however, they rebelled against God by choosing to eat the forbidden fruit—the knowledge of good and evil.

From that time on, every one of us has ratified that decision and has taken the same route. "Therefore, just as sin entered the world through one man, and death through sin, and in this way death came to all men, because all sinned" (Romans 5:12). It is people who are responsible for sin—not God.

But many ask, "Why didn't God make us so we couldn't sin?" To be sure, he could have, but let's remember that if he had done so we would no longer be human beings, we would be machines, mere puppets on a string. How would you like to be married to a mechanical doll? Every morning and every night you could pull the string and get the beautiful words, "I love you." But who would want that? There would never be any love, either. Love is voluntary. Our choices are voluntary. God could have made us like robots, but we would have ceased to be human. Would you like to be a robot? Few of us would honestly answer yes. God apparently thought it worth the risk of creating us as we are, and this is the reality we face.

> "As sure as I lived, I knew that I possessed a will . . . nobody else was making the choice for me."
>
> *Augustine of Hippo*

114

GOD COULD STAMP OUT EVIL!

Jeremiah reminds us, "Because of the Lord's great love we are not consumed, for his compassions never fail" (Lamentations 3:22). A time is coming when he will stamp out evil in the world. The devil and all his works will come under eternal judgment. In the meantime, God's unchanging love and grace prevail and his marvelous offer of mercy and pardon is still open to everyone.

If God were to stamp out evil today, he would do a complete job. We want him to stop war but stay remote from us. If God were to remove evil from the universe, his action would be complete and would have to include our lies and personal impurities, our lack of love and our failure to do good. Suppose God were to decree that tonight all evil would be removed from the universe—who of us would still be here after midnight?

The Bible tells us the sobering truth and explains: Sin has been passed on to all humankind through Adam and Eve's choice, and each of us has chosen to follow. From birth we begin by saying no. The sin of Adam and Eve separated them from the close relationship they had with God and does likewise for us. The perfect holiness of God could allow no less than separation. It is the consequence of our choices.

GOD'S ULTIMATE SOLUTION

In this dismal situation the loving God has done the most dramatic, costly and effective thing possible by giving his Son to die on our behalves. It is possible for people to escape God's inevitable judgment on sin and evil. It also possible to have its power broken by entering into a personal relationship with the Lord Jesus Christ. The ultimate answer to the problem of evil, at the personal level, is found in the sacrificial death of Jesus Christ.

To speculate about the origin of evil is endless. No one has the full answer. It belongs in the category of "the secret things [that] belong to the LORD our God" (Deuteronomy 29:29).

Hugh Evan Hopkins observes:

> The problem (of evil) arises largely from the belief that a good God would reward each man according to his deeds and that an almighty God would have no difficulty in carrying this out. The fact that rewards and punishments, in the way of happiness and discomfort, appear to be haphazardly distributed in this life drives many to question either the goodness of God or his power.[1]

115

But would God be good if he were to deal with each person exactly according to his behavior? Consider what this would mean in your own life! The whole of the gospel as previewed in the Old Testament and broadcast in stereo in the New Testament is that God's goodness consists not only in his justice but also in his love, mercy and kindness. How thankful we and all people should be that "he does not treat us as our sins deserve or repay us according to our iniquities. For as high as the heavens are above the earth, so great is his love for those who fear him" (Psalm 103:10-11).

Such a concept of the goodness of God is also based on the faulty assumption that happiness is the greatest good in life. Happiness is usually thought of in terms of comfort. True, genuine, deep-seated happiness, however, is something much more profound than the ephemeral, fleeting enjoyment of the moment. And true happiness is not precluded by suffering. Sometimes, in his infinite wisdom, God knows that there are things to be accomplished in our character that can be brought only through suffering. To shield us from this suffering would be to rob us of a greater good.

EXACT REWARD CONCEPT

The apostle Peter refers to this when he says, "And the God of all grace, who called you to his eternal glory in Christ, after you have suffered a little while, will himself restore you and make you strong, firm and steadfast" (1 Peter 5:10).

To see the logical consequence of the exact reward concept, coined by John Stuart Mill, we need only turn to Hinduism. The law of karma says that all of the actions of life today are the result of the actions of a previous life. Blindness, poverty, hunger, physical deformity, isolation and other social agonies are all the outworking of punishment for evil deeds in a previous existence.

It would follow that any attempt to alleviate such pain and misery would be an interference with the just ways of God. This concept is one reason why the Hindus did so little for so long for their unfortunates. Some enlightened Hindus today are talking about and working toward social progress and change, but they have not yet reconciled this new concept with the clear, ancient doctrine of karma, which is basic to Hindu thought and life.

This karma concept attempts to give a neat, simple, clearly understood explanation of suffering: suffering is the result of previous evil-doing. Douglas Groothuis illustrates its weakness: If a child dying of leukemia is suffering because in a former life she slaughtered innocent people, she would not know of it. Nor would she be able to learn from it in her condition.

But does Christianity also hold that suffering is punishment from God? Certainly in the minds of many it does. "What did I do to deserve this?" is often the first question on the lips of a sufferer. And the conviction of friends, expressed or unexpressed,

One reason sin and suffering flourish results from sin's being treated like a cream puff instead of a rattlesnake.

116

frequently operates on this same assumption. The classic treatment of the problem of suffering and evil in the book of Job shows how this cruel assumption was wrongly accepted by Job's friends. It compounded his already staggering pain.

It is clear from the teaching of both the Old and the New Testaments that suffering may be the judgment of God, but there are many instances when it is totally unrelated to personal wrongdoing. An automatic assumption of guilt and consequent punishment is totally unwarranted.

God is not a sentimental grandfather in the sky with a boys-will-be-boys attitude. "A man reaps what he sows" (Galatians 6:7 is a solemn warning to any who would tweak God's nose in arrogant presumption. "One reason sin flourishes is that it is treated like a cream puff instead of a rattlesnake."[2]

That there may be a connection between suffering and sin is evident, but that it is not always so is abundantly clear. We have the unambiguous word of Jesus himself on the subject. The disciples apparently adhered to the direct retribution theory of suffering. One day when they saw a man who had been blind from birth they wanted to know who had sinned to cause this blindness—the man or his parents. Jesus made it clear that neither was responsible for his condition, "but this happened so that the work of God might be displayed in his life" (John 9:1-3).

On receiving word of some Galileans whom Pilate had slaughtered, Jesus went out of his way to point out that they were not greater sinners than other Galileans. He said that the eighteen people who had been killed when the tower of Siloam fell on them were not greater sinners than others in Jerusalem. From both incidents he made the point "Unless you repent, you too will all perish" (Luke 13:1-3).

Clearly, then, we are jumping the gun if we assume automatically, either in our own case or in that of another, that the explanation of any given tragedy or suffering is the judgment of God. Further, as Hopkins observes, it seems clear from biblical examples that if one's troubles are the just rewards of misdeeds, the sufferer is never left in any doubt when his trouble is a punishment.

JUDGMENT PRECEDED BY WARNING

Indeed, one of the profound truths of the whole of Scripture is that the judgment of God is preceded by warning. Throughout the Old Testament we have the repeated pleadings of God and warning of judgment. Only after warning is persistently ignored and rejected does judgment come. God's poignant words are an example. "I take no pleasure in the death of the wicked, but rather that they turn from their ways and live. Turn! Turn from your evil ways! Why will you die, O house of Israel?" (Ezekiel 33:11).

The same theme continues in the New Testament. What more moving picture of God's love and long-suffering is there than when Jesus wept over Jerusalem, "I have longed to gather your children together, as a hen gathers her chicks under her wings, but you were not willing" (Matthew 23:37). And we have the clear word of Peter that the Lord does not want "anyone to perish, but everyone to come to repentance" (2 Peter 3:9).

When someone asks, "How could a good God send people to hell?" we should point out that, in a sense, God sends no one to hell. We send ourselves. God has done all that is necessary for us to be forgiven, redeemed, cleansed and made fit for heaven. All that remains is for us to receive this gift. If we refuse it, God has no option but to give us our choice. For the person who does not want to be with God, even heaven would be hell.

> For the person who does not want to be with God, even heaven would be hell.

Though the judgment of God sometimes explains suffering, there are several other possibilities to consider. People, as we saw earlier, were responsible for the coming of sin and death into the universe. We must not forget that humankind's wrongdoing is also responsible for a great deal of misery and suffering in the world today. Negligence in the construction of a building has sometimes resulted in its collapse in a storm, with consequent death and injury. How many lives have been snuffed out by the murder of drunken driving? The cheating, lying, stealing and selfishness that are so characteristic of our society today all reap a bitter harvest of suffering. But we can hardly blame God for it! Think of all the misery that has its origin in the wrongdoing of human beings; it is remarkable how much suffering is accounted for in this way.

DOES THE DEVIL EXIST?

But we are not alone on this planet. By divine revelation we know of the presence of an "enemy," the devil. He appears in various forms, we are told, appropriate to the occasion. He may appear as an angel of light or as a roaring lion, depending on the circumstances and his purposes. His name is Satan. It was he whom God allowed to cause Job to suffer (Job 1:6-12). Jesus, in the parable of the Wheat and the Tares, explains the ruining of the farmer's harvest by saying, "An 'enemy' did this" (Matthew 13:28). Satan finds great pleasure in ruining God's creation and causing misery and suffering in people. God allows him limited power, but through the power of Jesus Christ, we have authority over Satan's power. "Resist the devil, and he will flee from you" (James 4:7), we are assured. Nevertheless, Satan accounts for some of the disease and suffering in the world today.

In answer to the question of why God allows Satan power to bring suffering, we can learn from Robinson Crusoe's answer to his man, Friday.

> "Well," says Friday, "you say God is so strong, so great; has he not as much strong, as much might as the devil?"
>
> "Yes, yes," says I; "Friday, God is much stronger than the devil."
>
> "But if God much strong, much might as the devil why God no kill the devil so make him no more do wicked?"
>
> "You may as well ask," answers Crusoe reflectively, "why does God *not* kill you and me when we do wicked things that offend him?"

119

GOD FEELS OUR SUFFERING

In considering pain and suffering, whether it is physical or mental, another important consideration must be kept in mind. God is not a distant, aloof, impervious potentate, far removed from his people and their sufferings. He not only is aware of suffering—he feels it.

No pain or suffering has ever come to us that has not first passed through the heart and hand of God. However greatly we may suffer, it is well to remember that God is the great sufferer. Comforting are the words of Isaiah the prophet, foretelling the agony of Christ: "He was despised and rejected by men, a man of sorrows, and familiar with suffering" (Isaiah 53:3). Another writer reminds us, "Because he himself suffered when he was tempted, he is able to help those who are being tempted" (Hebrews 2:18). And "We do not have a high priest who is unable to sympathize with our weaknesses, but we have one who has been tempted in every way, just as we are—yet was without sin" (Hebrews 4:15). Also we are told, "Do not grieve the Holy Spirit of God" (Ephesians 4:30).

The problem of evil and suffering is one of the profound problems of the ages. It is becoming increasingly acute in our time, with the threat of nuclear and biochemical war. There are no easy answers, and we do not have the last word. There are, however, clues.

RISKY GIFT OF FREE WILL

First, evil is a necessary part of free will. As J. B. Phillips put it:

> Evil is inherent in the risky gift of free will. God could have made us machines but to do so would have robbed us of our precious freedom of choice, and we would have ceased to be human. Exercise of free choice in the direction of evil in what we call the "fall" of man [Adam's sin in the garden of Eden] is the basic reason for evil and suffering in the world. It is man's responsibility, not God's. He could stop it, but in so doing would destroy us all. It is worth noting that the whole point of real Christianity lies not in interference with the human power to choose, but in producing a willing consent to choose good rather than evil.[3]

"In all their distress he [God] too was distressed ... in his love and mercy he redeemed them; he lifted them up and carried them all the days of old."

(Isaiah 60:9)

Unless the universe is without significance, the actions of every individual affects others. No one is an island. To have it otherwise would be like playing a game of chess and changing the rules after every move. Life would be meaningless.

Second, much of the suffering in the world can be traced directly to the evil choices men and women make. The suffering is often the logical consequence of these choices. This is quite apparent when a bank robber kills someone, but sometimes it is less apparent and more indirect, as when crooked decisions are made in government or business that may bring deprivation and suffering to many people unknown to those who make the decisions. Even the results of natural disasters are sometimes compounded by people's culpability in refusing to heed warnings of their coming.

Third, some but not all suffering is allowed by God as judgment and punishment. This is a possibility that must always be considered. God usually allows such suffering with a view to restoration and character formation, and those suffering as a result of their deeds usually know it (Hebrews 12:7-8, 11).

Fourth, God has a vengeful and implacable enemy in Satan, who was defeated at the cross but is free to work his evil deeds until the final judgment. That there is in the world a force of evil stronger than human beings is clear from revelation and from our own experience.

Fifth, God himself is the great sufferer and has fully met the problem of evil in the gift of his own Son, at infinite cost and suffering to himself. The consequence of evil for eternity is forever removed as we embrace the Lord Jesus Christ. Our sin is forgiven, and we receive new life and power to choose what is God's best way for us. He directs us and strengthens us and forms us to be more like Jesus Christ in our character.

GREATEST TEST OF FAITH

God's pledge is not that suffering will never afflict us but that it will never separate us from his love.

Perhaps the greatest test of faith for the Christian today is to believe that God is good. There is much in our lives and culture that, taken in isolation, suggests the contrary. Helmut Thielecke points out that a fabric viewed through a magnifying glass is clear in the middle and blurred at the edges. Because of what we see in the middle, we know for certain the edges are clear. Life, he says, is like viewing a fabric.

Around the many edges of our lives, much is blurred, many events and circumstances we do not understand. But they can be interpreted rightly by the clarity we see in the center—the cross of Christ. We are not left to guess about the goodness of God from isolated bits of data. He has clearly revealed his character and dramatically demonstrated it to us in the cross. "He who did not spare his own Son, but gave him up for us all—how will he not also, along with him, graciously give us all

121

things?" (Romans 8:32).

God never asks us to understand but just to trust him in the same way we ask our child to trust our love and care when we take her to a doctor. Peace comes when we recognize that in this life we do not have the full picture. Yet we do have enough to show us the edges will be great.

We can affirm, with calm relief and joy, that in "all things God works for the good of those who love him" (Romans 8:28).

At times it is our reaction to suffering, rather than the suffering itself, that determines whether the experience is one of blessing or of blight. The same sun melts the butter and hardens the clay.

When by God's grace we can view all of life through the lens of faith in God's love, we can affirm with Habakkuk, "Though the fig tree does not bud and there are no grapes on the vines, though the olive crop fails and the fields produce no food, though there are no sheep in the pen and no cattle in the stalls, yet I will rejoice in the LORD, I will be joyful in God my Savior" (Habakkuk 3:17-18).

FOR FURTHER READING

Lewis, C. S. *The Problem of Pain*. New York: Simon & Schuster, 1996.

Lloyd-Jones, Martyn D. *Why Does God Allow Suffering?* Wheaton, Ill.: Crossway, 1994.

Yancey, Philip. *Where Is God When It Hurts?* Grand Rapids, Mich.: Zondervan, 1977.

CHAPTER ELEVEN

DOES CHRISTIANITY DIFFER FROM OTHER WORLD RELIGIONS?

How Christianity differs significantly from other religions is a subject often discussed in our shrinking world. We see a mixture of cultures, nations, races and religions on a scale unprecedented in history. We require no more than twenty-four hours to reach any spot on earth from our local airports. Television brings into our living rooms the Dalai Lama seen in Pakistan, Muslims bowing in Iran, and racial and religious wars in Africa.

Over 563,000 students and postdoctoral scholars from over 212 countries of the world came to the United States in the year 1996-1997 to study in more than 2,428 colleges and universities in every one of the fifty states.[1] Brightly colored saris on graceful Indian women and striking turbans on erect Sikhs are not unfamiliar sights in local malls and small college towns. In addition, thousands of diplomats, businesspeople and tourists come to America every year.

These newcomers find their way into parent-teacher meetings, service clubs and churches to speak on their cultural and religious backgrounds. They are sincere, educated and intelligent. They are often interested in learning about Christianity, and we can learn from them.

IS CHRISTIANITY UNIQUE?

As we have contact with these friends from overseas, their religious beliefs naturally raise questions for all of us as to whether or not Christianity is true. Is it unique among world religions? Or is it simply a variation on a basic theme running through all religions? To put it another way, "Does not the sincere Muslim, Buddhist, Hindu or Jew worship the same God as we do but under a different name?" Or, quite bluntly, "Is Jesus Christ the only way to God?"

When the Bible asserts that Jesus Christ is the only way to God and that apart from him there is no salvation, this could leave the impression Christians are bigoted, closed in their thinking. Or worse, Christians think they are better than anyone else. It sounds as if Christians have their own private bigots club, like a fraternity with a racial segregation clause. Actually, in every area of life it's easy to subtly give the impression that we are asking, "Why aren't you normal like me?"

It's common to hear statements like, "Just let everyone believe in God"; "Why bring Jesus into it?"; "Agree on God—that's enough." But can Christianity blend in with other religions and drop being exclusive?

THE CRUX OF THE MESSAGE

Fundamentally, for the Christian, it is impossible to be theologically inclusive. The cornerstone of the Christian message is Jesus Christ—God come to earth. Without this basis, any other parts lack meaning. Multiple verses in the New Testament give this basic thought. I'll quote three of them here: *"Salvation is found in no one else, for there is no other name under heaven given to men by which we must be saved"* (Acts 4:12, emphasis added). The apostle John said, "No one has ever seen God, but *God the One and Only, who is at the Father's side, has made him known"* (John 1:18, emphasis added). Jesus made his summary statement, *"I am the way, the truth and the life. No one comes to the Father except through me"* (John 14:6, emphasis added).

Christians believe this not because they have made it their rule but because Jesus Christ and the Bible, their source, states it. In fact, this core message is woven through both the Old and New Testaments. Christians are not giving their own bias but are explaining the biblical facts.

If we should say we would like to change this truth and vote in something more inclusive, here is our dilemma. We would be changing something that is not humanly changeable. It is fixed and is either completely true or completely false. It is "true-truth," as Francis Schaeffer stated it.

• There are some laws or truths *we could change*. For instance, the penalty for driving through a stoplight is determined by society's vote. It is not inherent in the act itself. The penalty, likewise, could be set at fifty dollars or at ten dollars, or the law could be abolished completely.

124

> The uniqueness of Christ is threefold:
> • his Incarnation—God come to earth
> • his death, "the just One for the unjust" on the cross
> • his rising again to authenticate who he was and why he came

• Other laws, like gravity, are irrevocable truths *we cannot change.* They are not socially determined no matter what the opinion polls or culture. Truth is solid, fixed and certain. The penalty is also not socially determined. People could vote unanimously to suspend the law of gravity for an hour, but no one in his right mind would jump off the roof to test it! No, the penalty for violating gravity is inherent in the act itself, and the person who violated it would be picked up with a blotter despite the unanimous resolution!

• As there are inherent physical laws, so there are *inherent spiritual laws.* One of them is God's initiative and revealing himself in Jesus Christ's coming to earth. Another is Christ's death as the route to forgiveness of sins and beginning a one-on-one relationship with God. To talk about the exclusiveness of Christ, a Christian is not assuming a superior posture in any way. There is no room for arrogance. Rather, it is a person whose life has been touched by God's intervention and grace. D. T. Niles describes Christians telling their personal stories: "It is just one beggar telling another beggar where to find food."

125

IS SINCERITY ENOUGH?

Having seen that spiritual truth is not arrived at by a majority vote, a general consideration of truth does help. To begin with, *sincerely believing something* does not make it true, as anyone will testify who has ever picked a wrong bottle out of a medicine cabinet in the dark. We've previously said faith is no more valid than the object in which it is placed. It doesn't matter how sincere or how intense the faith. A nurse put carbolic acid in the eyes of a newborn baby, sincerely thinking she was applying silver nitrate. Her sincerity did not save the baby from blindness.

These same principles apply to things spiritual. *Believing something doesn't make it true any more than failing to believe truth makes it false.* Facts are facts, regardless of people's attitudes toward them. In religious matters, the basic question is always, "Are the facts true?"

Ravi Zacharias gives helpful insight on the laws of logic. First, there is the either/or principle, the law of noncontradiction. Jesus Christ is God *or* not God: true *or* not true. If Jesus Christ is God, Brahma or one of the 330 million gods cannot also truly be God. If Jesus Christ was the author of creation, as the Bible teaches, it was not Brahma. It was either one or the other. Think back: the carbolic acid was either poisonous or not!

This logic would be like my saying "There is no bus coming. I will cross the street." But you would say, "There *is* a bus coming. I will not cross." We would know the truth when I cross the street. One must be true and the other not.

The opposite logic would be the both/and principle. This would say that both Brahma and Jesus are truly God, the polytheistic view. "Have as many Gods as you want" goes along with this view.[2]

The application of the both/and principle leads to an impasse in our thinking. Consider creation, for instance. Which God or gods created the world? Which God will tell me truth about life? Which one shall I pray to? How do I know which one is good and which one is not? Can there be Jesus and a plethora of other gods?

Take, for instance, the fact of the deity, death and resurrection of Jesus Christ. Christianity affirms these facts as the heart of its message. Islam, on the other hand, denies the deity, death and resurrection of Christ. On this very crucial point, one of these mutually contradictory views is *untrue and wrong.* They cannot both be simultaneously true, no matter how sincerely each is believed by any number of people.

A great deal is said about the similarity of world religions. Many Christians naively assume that other religions are basically the same, making the same claims and essentially doing what Christianity does but in slightly different terms. It would seem that such an attitude of using the both/and principle makes all religions identical, for example, "Both Islam and Christianity are true" (although Muslims would also strongly disagree with this).

"Add another God" would be another application of the both/and principle. There may be some similarities between religions but *the differences far outweigh them.*

IS THE GOLDEN RULE ENOUGH?

One of the similarities is the belief in the Golden Rule, which is contained in almost every religion. From Confucius's time we have the statement, in various forms: do unto others as we would have others do unto us. This is sometimes assumed to be the essence of Christianity. If all Jesus Christ did was give us the Sermon on the Mount and the Golden Rule, he would have actually increased our frustration. Few of us can consistently keep these. Our problem has never been *not knowing what we should do.* Our problem, rather, has been *lacking the power,* the ability, to do what we know is helpful, moral, good, just, honest and kind.

Jesus Christ not only taught the Golden Rule; he came to help us keep it. This is the major distinction between Christianity and other religions. He offers us his power to live as we should, gives us forgiveness as a free gift. He gives us his "new" life, his own righteousness. We can start over again. He does something for us we cannot do for ourselves.

BASIC CHRISTIANITY

If this list of God's actions seems too good to be true, a brief look at God's character is our starting point for basic Christianity. Mark Mittelberg and Bill Hybels in their book *Becoming a Contagious Christian* explain three seminal characteristics of God:

> First of all, God is *loving.* Out of His compassion He made us and desires to have a relationship with us. He continues to patiently extend His love to us. Many people prefer to stop here, but there's more that needs to be said.
>
> Secondly, you see, God is *holy.* This means that He is absolutely pure and he is separate from everything that is impure.
>
> The third characteristic of God is He is *just.* In other words, He is like a good judge who can't wink at a broken law: rather, He must mete out justice.[3]

The most difficult thing for us to comprehend is God's total separateness from us compared to our standard of holiness. When we rise in anger over senseless and vicious acts on the helpless, we experience an inkling of his abhorrence of evil. "He cannot even look at evil," the Bible asserts. It is God's nature to be righteous and just. God's infinite holiness far exceeds ours, like comparing the difference between the top of the tallest tree as our standard of holiness and the moon as God's standard.

One college graduate told me soberly, "If God grades on the curve, I'll be okay." He felt he was about average in his life and morals. God to him was a professor with set guidelines, and he came out average.

To get a brief summary of the heart of biblical Christianity we will look at the most universally quoted verse in the Bible—John 3:16.

• *"God so loved the world,"* each one of us whom he created. The words "so loved" mean that God loves us more than a mother cares for a child or a father slaves to support his family. God cares for each of us.

• *"He gave his one and only Son, Jesus Christ"* to come to earth, "to rescue us," to be our "truth and life." All of our ethical and moral remedies have failed. We have turned away from God's way. We need a Savior. This is not our struggling toward God, but God reaching down for us. He knew more rules would not help.

Instead the holy and just God came to earth, and was called Jesus, "for he will save his people from their sins" (Matthew 1:21).

• *"That whoever believes in him"*—the offer is open to all. Anyone who will come, he lovingly receives. Whoever says to him "Yes, I need you" will know he answers. He brings divine help and forgiveness. He gives a whole new life and cements a relationship with himself. Give yourself to him and you will find your real self, as your Creator intended you to be.

• *"Shall not perish but have eternal life."* He rescues you, "saves" you from "perishing" for your sins and failures. You will be forgiven, freed from binding habits, from persistent emptiness and repetitious guilt. Even those "little sins" of the generally moral person will be forgiven. Eternal life is God's life that he gives us. "A new person," the apostle Paul calls it. Whatever our circumstances, he receives us and gladly rescues us from the seas of uncertainty and emptiness. Imagine life with your hand in his hand each day!

Receiving him into your life is not a do-it-yourself proposition. It is not saying, "Work hard at it and follow this way and you will gain favor with God." It is not a set of swimming instructions for a drowning man. Jesus Christ himself comes to be our life preserver.

A FREE GIFT

A "life preserver" is one who jumps in, helps and saves. Jesus described his coming as "giving his life a ransom for many." He is God-come-to-earth alongside us to help. D. T. Niles explains that in other religions people are left to do the best they can, follow the rules and do "good works." These are all "in order to" gain their own particular promised goal (and every religion has some promised utopia and euphoria that is offered).

> God became man to turn creatures into children, not simply to produce better of the old kind of people but to produce a new kind of person.

Mark Mittelberg clarifies the difference between religion and Christianity. "Religion is spelled 'Do,' because it consists of the things people *do* to try to somehow gain God's forgiveness and favor. . . . Thankfully Christianity is spelled differently. It's spelled 'D-O-N-E.'"[4]

For the Christian, doing good deeds is the result of gratitude for the Savior who became our life preserver. They are an expression of gratitude and commitment to follow his guidance.

The mystery of God's love and Jesus' coming as our Rescuer is found in his final death on the cross. This innocent God-man was cruelly slaughtered and took the punishment that all sin rightly deserved. It was the punishment that you and I deserve. At the cross alone the love and justice of God are bound together. Here our moral and human failures can be declared forgiven. The cross speaks the message of love and forgiveness whether seen on a church tower or jewelry counters: love and justice are satisfied. William Lane Craig tells a story of three men's reactions when they finally saw Christ's reality.

> Three men stood in a crowd before God's throne on the Judgment day. Each had a score to settle with God. "I was hanged for a crime I didn't commit," complained one man bitterly. "I died from a disease that dragged on for months, leaving me broken in body and spirit," said another. "My son was killed in a prime of life when some drunk behind the wheel jumped the curb and ran him down," muttered the third. Each was angry and anxious to give God a piece of his mind. But when they reached the throne and saw their Judge with his nail-scarred hands and feet and his wounded side, each mouth was stopped. They dropped silently to their knees at the sight of their Savior.[5]

THREE MAJOR RELIGIONS

From this picture of God's gift, we will briefly contrast three other major world religions. What their view of salvation is and what they are pointing toward will be seen as quite different from the picture we have drawn so far.

• *Buddhism* began with Gautama Siddhartha, born 563 B.C. in northern India. He, like other seekers of his day, launched upon a pilgrimage of inquiry in search of answers to suffering and the way to peace. Finally, he felt he achieved "the great enlightenment" and experienced "nirvana" or supreme blessedness. This experience shaped his thoughts, became widely taught, and he became known as "the Buddha," or "the enlightened one."

Nirvana he described as a state achieved by extinction of the individual's existence through the absorption of the soul into the supreme spirit. Reaching nirvana is likened to the blowing out of a candle (self-annihilation or total nothingness). Buddha's diagnosis was his four basic "noble truths": (1) suffering is universal, (2) the cause of suffering is desire—that eager grasping by the self, (3) the cure for suffering is the elimination of desire, and (4) desire is eliminated by following his Eightfold Path to Enlightenment.

The Eightfold Path, common to all Buddhism, includes right knowledge, right feeling, right speech, right action, right living, right effort, right insight and right meditation. Elimination of desire is the central theme and goal to bring a person to nirvana—ultimate bliss achieved by absorption of the individual into the supreme oneness of the universe—again, like the blowing out of a candle.

In addition, Buddha accepted the ironclad law of cause and effect known as karma, that is, all actions have an effect, either good or bad in this life or the next rebirth. The belief in successive lives or transmigration of the soul to another earthly life will be determined by our actions in this life. This specifically implies the passing of the "spark" of life or the soul to become at death some other body or form. Buddha's intent was evidently to help his followers escape the cycle of suffering and desire through birth and rebirth.

• In *Hinduism* the ultimate goal is also nirvana, but the term here has a different meaning. Nirvana is ultimate reunion with Brahma, the all-pervading force of the universe that is the Hindu's chief of 330 million gods. This experience is likened to the return of a drop of water to the ocean. Individuality is lost in the reunion with their god, but without the total self-annihilation of a person's identity as taught in Buddhism.

Transcendental meditation or yoga is intended to bring a person into union with an impersonal universe or "god." Underlying these practices is a view of the sensory world as illusory. For the devout

Hindu, nirvana is achieved through a continuous cycle of birth, life, death and rebirth. As soon as any animal, insect or human being dies, that being is immediately reborn in another form. Whether one moves up or down the scale of life depends on the quality of moral life one has lived. If it has been a good life, one moves up the scale with more comfort and less suffering. If one has lived a bad life, one moves down the scale into suffering and poverty. If one has been bad enough, that person is not reborn as a human being at all but as an animal or insect.

This reaping in the next life the harvest of one's present life is also called the law of karma. It explains why Hindus will not kill even an insect, not to mention a sacred cow, though these inhibitions pose grave sanitation and public health problems. What seems strange and incomprehensible to someone in the Western world has a very clear rationale to the Hindu.

• In *Islam,* heaven is thought of as a paradise of pleasure and indulgence. It is achieved by living a life of strict abstinence from self-indulgence of any kind while on earth. The teaching is that God (Allah) is an absolute unity and the Creator and sovereign Lord of the universe. He is also the ultimate Judge of all people. Muhammad, the prophet of Allah, rejected the idea that Jesus, a human being, could be God. Jesus is hailed as a great prophet of Allah but not as God incarnate.

Five duties are the pillars of Islam. They include repeating a creed, making a pilgrimage to Mecca, giving alms to the poor, praying five times daily, and keeping the fast of Ramadan (one month of fasting during the day).

131

These religions are different from Christianity in basic beliefs. These too imply the idea of *doing* as opposed to the cross of Christ *rescuing* and *forgiving* us. Again, there is no possibility of assurance. I have often asked Hindus, Muslims and Buddhists if they will achieve nirvana or go to paradise when they die. I have not yet had one reply in the affirmative. Rather, they referred to the imperfection of their lives as being a barrier to this realization. There is no assurance in their belief systems. Consequently, salvation depends wholly on an individual's working to gain merit.

In his book *The Abolition of Man,* C. S. Lewis points out that there is moral instruction of some kind in every religion. But in Christianity the significant and important difference is in the living Christ. His Spirit, given to each one who believes, provides the power to obey God's teachings and comes to those who believe in God's Son and open themselves to his leading.

CONCEPT OF GOD

Even the fundamental concept of God, on which there is a plea that we should agree, reveals wide divergences. To say that we can unite with all who believe in God, regardless of what this God is called, fails to recognize that the term *God* means nothing apart from the definition given it.

Buddha, contrary to popular belief, never claimed to be deity. In fact, he was agnostic about the whole question of whether God even existed. If God existed, the Buddha taught emphatically that he could not help an individual achieve enlightenment. Each person must work this out for himself or herself.

Hindu teaching is pantheistic. *Pan* means "all" and *theistic* refers to "God." Hindus believe that God and the universe are identical. The concept of *maya* is central to their thinking. *Maya* is the dualistic perception that the physical world is an illusion: we think we are personal beings, but we are not; we suffer because we think we are personal, but we are not. To this philosophy, all thinking and feeling is illusory. Reality is instead spiritual and invisible. Brahma is the ultimate reality, the Universal Soul. Every person—indeed, everything that exists—is Brahman since all is god.

Buddhism also teaches that the material world is an illusion. It is readily apparent why modern science came to birth through Christians, who believed in a personal God and an orderly universe, rather than in the context of Eastern philosophy. This explains why most scientific progress has come from the West rather than the East. Why would a person investigate what he believes is an illusion?

In Islam and Judaism we have a God much closer to the Christian concept. Here God is personal and transcendent—separate from his creation. Surely, we are urged, we may get together with those who believe in God in personal terms.

But as we examine the Muslim concept of God—Allah, as he is called in the Qur'an—we find he is not the God and Father of Jesus Christ but rather a God who is utterly transcendent. Knowledge of Allah comes from the Qur'an, which came through Muhammad. He taught that he was the final prophet of Allah.

The picture of God in the Qur'an is of one who is totally removed from people, one who is capricious in all of his acts, responsible for evil as well as for good, and who is certainly not the God who "so loved the world that he gave his one and only Son." It is a totally distant concept of God that makes the idea of the incarnation of Jesus

Christ utterly inconceivable to the Muslim. How could their god, so majestic and beyond, have contact with mortal human beings in sin and misery? The death of God the Son on the cross is likewise inconceivable to a Muslim, since this would mean God was defeated by his creatures, an impossibility to them.

Buddhism	essentially agnostic regarding the existence and character of God
Hinduism	basically pantheistic—God is in everything—but also polytheistic, reporting 330 million gods (including Jesus)
Islam	monotheistic like Christianity, but rejects Jesus as the incarnation of God

Table 11.1. Views of God: A summary

THE JEWISH GOD IS CLOSE

The Jewish concept of God is closest of all to the Christian. Isn't the God whom they worship the God of the Old Testament, which we accept? Surely we can get together on this!

Again, however, closer examination shows that the majority of Jews do not admit their God is the Father of Jesus Christ. Some may believe Jesus was a great man, but not their Messiah (Savior). In fact, it was this very issue that precipitated such bitter controversy in Jesus' time. God we accept, they said to Jesus Christ, but we do not accept you because as a man you are claiming yourself to be God. This, in their view, is a clear case of blasphemy.

In a conversation with the Jewish religious leaders, Jesus discussed this question. "God is our Father," they said. Jesus said to them, "If God were your Father, you would love me, for I came from God. . . . He who belongs to God hears what God says. The reason you do not hear is that you do not belong to God" (John 8:42, 47).

It is quite obvious the Jewish leaders were not sincere seekers. If people are seeking the true God, their sincerity will be evident and their efforts rewarded. Missionary history has numerous examples of those who have been following other gods or an unknown god but who have responded when presented with the truth about Jesus Christ. His message opens their understanding that he is the true God, whom they have been seeking.

JESUS CHRIST ALONE CLAIMS DEITY

Of the great religious leaders of the world, Christ alone claims deity. It really doesn't matter what one thinks of Muhammad, Buddha or Confucius as individuals. Their followers emphasize their teachings. Not so with Christ. He made himself the focal point of his teaching. The central question he put to his listeners was, "Who do you say that I am?" When asked what doing the works of God involved, Jesus replied, "The work of God is this: to believe in the one he has sent" (John 6:29).

On the question of who and what God is, the nature of salvation and how it is obtained, it is clear that Christianity differs radically from other world religions. We live in an age in which tolerance is a key word. Tolerance, however, must be clearly understood. (Truth, by its very nature, is intolerant of error.) If two plus two is four, the total at the same time cannot be twenty-three. But one is not regarded as intolerant because he disagrees with this answer and maintains that the only correct answer is four.

The same principle applies in religious matters. One must be tolerant of other points of view and respect their right to be held and heard. We cannot, however, be forced in the name of tolerance to agree that all points of view are equally valid, including those that are mutually contradictory. This would be nonsense.

134

THE ONLY WAY TO GOD

It is not true that "it doesn't matter what you believe as long as you believe it." Hitler's slaughter of six million Jews was based on a sincere view of race supremacy, but he was desperately wrong. What we believe must be true in order to be real. Again, Jesus said, "I am the way and the truth and the life. No one comes to the Father except through me" (John 14:6). If we are to know the true and living God in personal experience, it will be through Jesus Christ.

FOR FURTHER READING

Anderson, Norman. *Christianity and World Religions.* 2nd ed. Downers Grove, Ill.: InterVarsity Press, 1984.

Corduan, Winfried. *Neighboring Faiths.* Downers Grove, Ill.: InterVarsity Press, 1998.

Enroth, Ronald M. *A Guide to Cults and New Religions.* Downers Grove, Ill.: Inter-Varsity Press, 1984.

Sire, James W. *The Universe Next Door: A Basic Worldview Catalog.* Downers Grove, Ill.: InterVarsity Press, 1997.

CHAPTER TWELVE

IS CHRISTIAN
EXPERIENCE VALID?

"You could get the same response from that table lamp if you believed it possessed the same attributes as your God," said the young law student. This articulate skeptic was telling me what thousands feel—that Christian experience is completely personal and subjective and has no objective, eternal and universal validity.

The premise behind this notion is that the mind is capable of infinite rationalization. Belief in God is seen as mere wish fulfillment. In adults, it is a throwback to our need for a father image.

The assumption, whether expressed or not, is that Christianity is for emotional cripples who can't make it through life without a crutch.

It is claimed that Christian conversion is a psychologically induced experience brought about by brainwashing. An evangelist is just a master of psychological manipulation. After pounding away at an audience, he finds that people become putty in his hands. He can get them to do anything if he asks for a decision at the right time and in the right way.

Some go further. Christian experience, they claim, is sometimes downright harmful. More than one student has been packed off to a psychiatrist by unbelieving parents after he or she has come to personal faith in Christ. "Look at all the religious nuts in mental asylums. It's their religion that put them there." Those who feel this way have succumbed to the "common-factor fallacy" pointed out by Anthony Standen. He tells of a man who got drunk each Monday on whiskey and soda water; on Tuesday he got drunk on brandy and soda water; and Wednesday on gin and soda water. What caused the drunkenness? Obviously the common factor, soda water![1]

THE LAST STOP ON THE TRAIN

For many, the church is thought of as the last stop on the train before being institutionalized. A careful scrutiny of a truly disoriented person, however, would reveal imbalance and unreality in other areas as well as in their religious life. It is actually a credit to the church that she offers help to all people regardless of their situation. There is no doubt that some emotional disturbances may have spiritual roots. Regardless of the challenges that face any of us, opening our lives to a relationship with God through Jesus Christ can bring release and healing.

So strong is the prejudice in some quarters against the validity of the Christian experience that academic degrees have been denied. A friend, studying in one of our best-known universities, was denied a Ph.D. degree in social science. He was told, "Believing what you do about God, you are by definition crazy."

I've heard some skeptics suggest that all Christian experience can be explained on the basis of conditioned reflexes. This thinking has its roots in experiments by Pavlov, the famous Russian scientist. He placed measuring devices in a dog's mouth and stomach to determine the production of digestive juices. Then he would bring food to the dog and at the same time ring a bell. After doing this repeatedly over a period of time, Pavlov rang the bell without producing the food and the dog salivated as usual. The inference drawn is that by such repeated conditioning, the mind can be made to produce desired physical reactions. It is on this basis that we can explain all political, social and religious conversions, say the proponents of this view.

These are serious, far-reaching charges, and some of them have an air of plausibility.

IS THE CHRISTIAN EXPERIENCE VALID?

At the outset we must concede the possibility of manipulating human emotions in some circumstances. And we would have to admit that some teachers or preachers consciously or unconsciously play on the emotions of their audiences with deathbed stories, histrionic performances and other devices.

Jesus, in the parable of the Sower, implicitly warns against merely stirring the emotions. He describes the times when someone hears "the Word" and likens the Christian message to a seed that falls on stony places. At first the message is received with joy but roots never grow deep inside. The hearers endure for a while, but when difficulty comes, there is no clear belief. They get turned off and fall by the wayside.

The implication is that when we hear about God and Jesus Christ, our emotions can be moved. If and when hard times come, the rose-colored glasses come off. Life in general is solving problems, we discover. And "not every day is a three-cookie day," to quote Max Lucado. Emotions are undulant and may even vary with the weather. The good news is that Christian truth does not rest on emotional highs. At times of uncertainty it is helpful to review the facts, and we will find an even deeper faith will result.

A MATTER OF THE WILL

Orville S. Walters, a Christian psychiatrist, has pointed out that the will is like a cart pulled by two horses—the emotions and the intellect. With some people the will (the cart) responds more quickly through the emotions. With others the will (the cart) is reached through the mind. But in every case genuine faith involves a decision of the will.[2]

137

We admit the potentialities for transient emotional response, but we cannot explain all Christian experience on a psychological basis. It does not fit the facts. We do well to observe a principle that applies here as well as in other areas: to describe something is not the same thing as explaining it. To be sure, Christian experience can be described psychologically, but this does not explain *why* it happens nor negate its reality.

We have described the reality of God's true love for us, unmerited and unearned. The experience of assurance and acceptance can bring joy and inner contentment. One sage said, "Taste and see that the LORD is good" (Psalm 34:8). Verify for yourself, in the laboratory of life, the hypothesis that Jesus Christ is the living Son of God. Coupled with its twin truth of God's objective revelation, the personal Christian experience assures us of the trustworthiness of the message.

A CONDITIONED REFLEX?

What of the objections that Christian experience is merely a conditioned reflex?

First, can the comparison between people and animals be a legitimate one? A human being has reason and a critical faculty, and has powers of self-analysis, self-contemplation and self-criticism that make him or her quite different from animals. D. Martyn Lloyd-Jones's answer to the influential book *Battle for the Mind* by William Sargant states: "In other words, the comparison is only valid at times (like war) when what differentiates man has been knocked out of action and a man, because of terrible stress, has been reduced for the time being to the level of an animal."[3]

Second, if we are only creatures of conditioned reflexes, then this must also explain acts of great heroism and self-sacrifice in which human beings have taken pride. Such acts must be nothing but responses to a given stimulus at a given point. Taken to its logical conclusion, a deterministic view of human behavior eliminates moral responsibility—what's going to happen will happen and I can't change it. Or what happens "ain't my fault; it's my genes." Those holding a deterministic point of view philosophically tend to deny this fatalistic position in their everyday daily practices. Like anyone else, they want a thief arrested promptly if they are the ones stolen from.

Conditioned reflex does not explain the vast number who tell of their undeniable Christian experience. Thousands reared in Christian homes unfortunately never become Christians. Thousands of others with no background or knowledge of the faith have become Christians. I have known people who became Christians the first time they heard God's story and human salvation. By contrast, others have studied the evidence repeatedly before deciding to trust Christ.

There are those who have become Christians out of every conceivable (or no prior) religious background. Each testifies uniformly to a personal inner confirmation. Wholehearted commitment to Jesus Christ brought a confirming, subjective experience. A visibly changed life is not phony or superficial. Thousands of stories could be told as well as read.

Such results would not be gained from a table lamp by positive thinking. A "positive object" is imperative, one more substantial than a lamp! Positive thinking alone is far distant from faith in a living Creator who cares for us. I was very thankful the law student previously referred to committed his life to Christ in the course of the week's lectures that followed.

Victims of Autohypnosis?

But how would we know when considering Christianity whether or not we are victims of autohypnosis? How would we know we are not just whistling in the dark? Subjective experience as such does not prove anything. Many have claimed to experience a reality that we may legitimately question. Again, there must be more than experience on which to base our convictions, or we could be in difficulty.

For instance, suppose a man with a fried egg over his left ear came through the door of a church. "Oh," he says, glowing, "this egg really gives me joy, peace, purpose in life, forgiveness of sins and strength for living!" What would you say to him? You can't tell him he hasn't experienced these things. One of the powers of personal testimony is that it cannot be argued. The blind man whom Jesus healed couldn't answer many of the questions put to him, but he was sure of the fact that now he could see (see John 9). His testimony was eloquent in its power.

But we could ask several questions of our friend with the fried egg. These are questions Christians must also be prepared to answer.

First, who else has had the same experience with the fried egg? Presumably our friend would be hard put to produce others. The late Harry Ironside was preaching some years ago when a heckler shouted, "Atheism has done more for the world than Christianity!"

"Very well," said Ironside, "tomorrow night you bring a hundred men whose lives have been changed for the better by atheism, and I'll bring a hundred who have been transformed by Christ."

139

Needless to say, his heckler friend did not appear the next night. With Christianity there are people from every race, every country and every walk of life who bear testimony to an experience through Jesus Christ.

Second, we should ask our friend with the fried egg: What objective reality outside of himself is his internal subjective experience tied to? How does he know he is not a victim of autohypnosis? Of course he will have nothing to say. In Christianity a personal subjective experience is tied to the objective historical fact of the resurrection of Christ. If Christ had not risen from the dead, we would not experience him. It's because he rose from the dead and is living today that we can actually know him.

Objective Historical Fact

Christian experience is not induced by belief in unrealities. It is not like the fraternity boy who died of fright when tied to a railroad track one night during hazing. He was told that a train would be coming in five minutes. He was not told that the train would pass on a parallel track. He thought there was only one track. When he heard the train approaching he suffered heart failure. With Christianity, nothing happens if there is "no one out there."

Because Christ is really there, all the possibilities of his life within us are realizable. It is only half the story if we can say, "I know Jesus Christ has forgiven me." The other crucial half is that we know he lives because of the objective reality that he rose from the dead in history. Our personal subjective experience is based on objective historical fact.

In commenting on the truth that people in suffering speak of drawing upon power outside themselves, J. B. Phillips says:

> I know perfectly well that I am merely describing subjective phenomena. But the whole point is that what I have observed results in objective phenomena: courage, faith, hope, joy and patience, for instance, and these qualities are very readily observed. The man who wants everything proved by scientific means is quite right in his insistence on "laboratory conditions" if he is investigating, shall we say, water-divining, clairvoyance or telekinesis.

> But there can be no such thing as "laboratory conditions" for investigating the realm of the human spirit unless it can be seen that the "laboratory conditions" are in fact human life itself. A man can only exhibit objectively a change in his own disposition, a faith which directs his life in the actual business of living.[4]

Rich or poor, high or low, our needs are similar. Ravi Zacharias tells of an interview that David Frost conducted with billionaire Ted Turner. When unexpectedly asked if there was anything in his life he regretted, a sudden melancholic expression came on Turner's face. Somberly he answered, "Yes, the way I treated my first wife."[5]

It is in times of personal failures, regrets, or loss of any kind that the dynamic relevance of Christ can be experienced. He meets us in our deepest needs.

Purpose and Direction

Christ gives purpose and direction to life. "I am the light of the world," he says. "Whoever follows me will never walk in darkness but will have the light of life" (John 8:12). Many are in the dark about the purpose of life in general and about their own lives in particular. They are groping around the room of life looking for the light switch. Anyone who has ever been in a dark, unfamiliar room knows this feeling of insecurity. When the light goes on, however, a feeling of security results. And so it is when one steps from darkness to the light of life in Christ.

God in Christ gives our lives cosmic purpose, tying us in with his purpose for history and eternity. A Christian lives not only for time, but for eternity. Even routine is transformed as we live the whole of our lives in God's purpose and obey the admonition, "Whether you eat or drink or whatever you do, do it all for the glory of God" (1 Corinthians 10:31). This purpose embraces every aspect of life. It is also an unending, eternal purpose. Undoubtedly a non-Christian has such temporary purposes as family, career and money that give limited satisfaction. But these, at best, are transient and may fail with a change in circumstances.

To an age in which life has been described as meaningless and absurd by existentialist philosophers, nothing could have more power and meaning than this verifiable claim of Christ.

WE HAVE BEEN MADE FOR GOD

The late Carl Gustav Jung said, "The central neurosis of our time is emptiness." When we do not have money, fame, success, power and other externals, we think we'll achieve final happiness after we attain them. Many testify to the disillusionment experienced when these have been achieved and the realization sets in that one is still the same miserable person. The human spirit can never be satisfied "by bread alone" by material things. We have been made for God and can find rest only in him.

An automobile, however shiny, high-powered and full of equipment, will not run on water. It was made to run only on gasoline. So people can find fulfillment only in God. We were made this way by God himself. Christian experience offers this fulfillment in a personal relationship to Christ. He said, "I am the bread of life. He who comes to me will never go hungry, and he who believes in me will never be thirsty" (John 6:35). When one experiences Christ, he or she comes to an inner contentment, joy and spiritual refreshment that enables him or her to transcend circumstances. It was this reality that enabled Paul to say, "I have learned to be content whatever the circumstances" (Philippians 4:11).

This supernatural reality enables a Christian to rejoice in the middle of difficult circumstances.

OUR QUEST IS FOR PEACE

"Peace in our time" expresses the longing inside each of us as we view our own daily choices staring us in the face. Outside of ourselves we hope against hope that international terrorist wars will not erupt into larger conflicts.

Peace is the quest of every human heart. If it could be bought, people would pay millions for it. The skyrocketing sales of books dealing with peace of mind and soul testify that they have touched a resonant chord in the lives of millions. Psychiatrists' offices are jammed.

Jesus says, *"Come to me, all you who are weary and burdened, and I will give you rest"* (Matthew 11:28, emphasis added). Christ alone gives peace that passes understanding, a peace the world cannot give or take away. It is very moving to hear the life stories of those who have restlessly searched for years and have finally found peace in Christ. The current rise of relational breakups, families torn apart and hidden practices uncovered have found us searching in vain for peace in our time. We need not succumb to addictions of any form, visible sins or hidden hatreds and jealousies in the vain hope of gaining peace. There is one available and trustworthy haven of peace. Real, lasting peace comes from Christ alone; "He himself is our peace" (Ephesians 2:14).

A RADICAL POWER NEEDED

Today's society is experiencing a profound power failure, a moral power failure. Parents know what is right for themselves and their children, but in many cases they find it easier to go along with the crowd. Children readily pick up this attitude. The result is rapid deterioration of the moral fabric of society. Merely to give good advice to either the old or young is like putting iodine on cancer. What is needed is radical power.

Christianity is not the putting on of a new suit on a man but the putting of a new man into the suit. Jesus Christ said, "I have come that they may have life, and have it to the full" (John 10:10).

Jesus offers us his power. Not only is there power and freedom from any binding chains but power to forgive those who have wronged us, to love the unlovely and resist the temptation to retaliate. Twice-born people have new appetites, new desires, new loves. They

142

are, in fact, "new creations" (2 Corinthians 5:17). Again, newly believing people in reality have literally come from death to spiritual life.

GUILT AND LONELINESS PROBLEMS SOLVED

The Christian experience solves the guilt problem. Every normal person feels guilt. The guilt complex is an irrational feeling that has no basis in fact. But guilt felt over something done in violation of an inherent moral law is normal. The absence of any guilt feeling is abnormal. A person who feels nothing after deliberately killing or hurting an innocent person is abnormal. Guilt must not be rationalized away. In Christ there is an objective basis for forgiveness. Christ died for our sins; the sentence of death that belonged to us has been taken by him. "Therefore, there is now no condemnation for those who are in Christ Jesus" (Romans 8:1). Forgiveness at the personal level is a reality.

In the Spring term of university I gave in, and admitted that God was God and knelt and prayed; perhaps, that night, the most defected and reluctant convert in all England. I did not then see what is now the most shining and obvious thing; the Divine humility which will accept a convert even on such terms. The Prodigal Son at least walked home on his own feet. But who can duly adore that Love [of a Divine god] which will open the high gates to a prodigal who is brought in kicking, struggling, resentful, and darting his eyes in every direction for a chance of escape? But who can plumb the depth of the divine mercy? The hardness of God is kinder than the softness of men, and His compulsion is our liberation.

C. S. Lewis, *Surprised by Joy*

143

Christianity speaks to our loneliness, which is so characteristic of modern society. It is ironic that in a period of population explosion there are more lonely people than ever.

Christ is the Good Shepherd (John 10:14) who will never leave us nor forsake us. And he introduces us into a caring worldwide family.

New Birth Brings New Life

Finally, in recognizing the validity of Christian experience we should realize that a psychological description of it is valid as far as it goes. But it is only a description, not a cause. A person who comes to Jesus Christ and puts his or her life into Jesus' hands is "born anew" or "born of God," has God's Spirit, a new spiritual life within. This new life is likened to natural birth where a newborn baby will come alive, do new things and learn new things. There are a number of descriptions of "born anew" in the New Testament.

• "Everyone who believes that Jesus is the Christ is born of God." (1 John 5:1)

• "You have been born again, not of perishable seed, but of imperishable, through the living and enduring word of God." (1 Peter 1:17)

• "Therefore, if anyone is in Christ, he is a new creation." (2 Corinthians 5:17)

144

The next step is determining your own status with God, our magnificent Creator, and your individual relationship with him. You may have already made connection with him and his offer of "new life." Or you may need to take the next step. Decide to take action and personally seek him. Jesus sums up his coming with: "I am the door [likened to a sheep gate]. Whoever enters through me will be saved [born anew]" (John 10:9).

Have You Ever Personally Trusted Jesus Christ, or Are You Still on the Way?

A young man came to our home and asked me some hardball logical questions that bothered him about God and the Christian faith. We talked a long while until I finally asked him if he had ever personally put his life and trust in Jesus Christ. Very sincerely he replied, "I'm stuck between the screen door and the real door."

The whole issue could not have been expressed more clearly. Many are in the same place—still outside but down deep wanting to get in. The good news that day was that the young man decided he wanted to pray directly to God "in Jesus' name," as he put it. This was something he had never done before.

Bottom-line ingredients were in his prayer. He said:

> *First,* I know I need You, God, in my life. My sins are big and I need to be forgiven.
>
> *Second,* I ask you, God, through Jesus Christ, to guide my life, make it new and lead me in all the decisions I make.

Then he poured out spontaneously some of his inner battles, all with a kind of hope for freedom. At the end of the prayer, he whispered to the Lord, "Thanks."

He went through the door. And Jesus Christ was waiting for him. Incredibly, God is waiting for each of us.

FOR FURTHER READING

Farmer, Herbert H. "The Psychological Theory of Religion," in *Towards Belief in God.* New York: Macmillan, 1978.

Rowe, William L. "Freud and Religious Belief," in *Philosophy of Religion: An Introduction.* Belmont, Calif.: Wadsworth, 1978.

Schaeffer, Francis A. *The God Who Is There.* 30th anniv. ed. Downers Grove, Ill.: InterVarsity Press, 1999.

STUDY QUESTIONS

Chapter 1: *Is Christianity Rational?*

1. Centuries ago a person's faith in God was rarely challenged. Churches did almost nothing to encourage individuals to develop personal relationships with Christ. The church even withheld the Bible from popular use. Today's society often views a person's faith in God as a relic of the past. Yet Christians have more resources than ever before to help them develop a personal faith in Christ—millions of Bibles, thousands of churches and hundreds of religious radio and television programs. Do you think it is harder or easier to have a genuine, growing relationship with Christ now than it was in earlier centuries? Explain.

2. How specifically do you feel the world challenges your faith?

3. According to 1 Peter 3:15 we should "always be prepared to give an answer to everyone who asks you to give the reason for the hope that you have. But do this with gentleness and respect." Why would the Bible include such a command?

4. How would obeying this verse help to dispel the faulty concept in nonbelievers' minds that faith is "believing something you know isn't true"?

5. "Alleged intellectual problems are often a smoke screen covering moral rebellion" (p. 13). Do you agree or disagree? Why?

6. Because it would be easy to lump all skeptics into the category of morally rebellious smoke screeners, John Stott qualifies, "We cannot pander to a man's intellectual arrogance, but we must cater to his intellectual integrity" (p. 14). How would heeding this caution help a Christian treat each skeptic fairly and helpfully?

7. How do other factors (such as an abusive earthly father figure or emotional scars) affect one's ability to trust in God?

8. How are doubting Christians and skeptics usually handled in your fellowship group?

9. What is your usual response to the doubts of others—especially Christians who have professed faith for some time?

10. Is there a group in your church in which "doubters" can discuss their problems in an unhurried, nonthreatening way? If not, and you think such a group would be of value, how could you help get one started?

11. Think of someone who genuinely seems open to trusting Christ yet is still having a problem believing. What reasons might cause this? How could you help the person through the roadblocks?

12. Peter's encouragement to us to be prepared to give an answer for the hope that is in us is worth following through on. So as you work your way through this book, take time to compile a list of such reasons. You can start with any you have found in the course of reading this chapter.

> **God's love is more than you think.**

Chapter 2: *Is There a God?*

1. What, according to the author, must occur for something to be scientifically proven (p. 18)?

2. Why can't the existence of God be proven in this way?

3. According to anthropology all of the world's cultures originally believed in one God who was the creator. Why would atheists feel they had the upper hand if they could prove this were not so?

4. Summarize the evidence for God's existence based on the law of cause and effect and the

fact of the universe's apparent order and design (p. 19).

5. What do you think of the theory of "infinite time plus chance" (pp. 19-21)? What would you say to someone who believed this theory?

6. What is the "moral argument" for the existence of God (pp. 25-26)?

7. How would you argue for or against the "moral argument"?

8. Paul Little offers the evidence of "changed lives" as further proof of God's existence (p. 28). Because this evidence is subjective, it could be hard to prove and easy to counterfeit. Would the testimony of a born-again Christian sound very different from a person whose life was transformed by newfound faith in another religion? Why or why not?

9. If you were to give "changed lives" as an evidence of God's existence, what personal evidence would you be able to offer?

10. What other arguments for or against the existence of God can you think of?

11. Which of the arguments for God's existence seem most helpful to you in explaining the plausibility of God's existence? Why?

12. Which ones seem least helpful? Why?

13. If you would like to gain experience explaining the evidence for God's existence, think of someone who may be interested in hearing your reasons for believing. Consider setting up a time to talk to that person about your reasons for believing in God.

14. Take time now to add any new insights to your list of reasons for putting your hope in God through Christ Jesus.

> **Nothing produces nothing. If the concept of God is unthinkable, it makes sense for us to rethink our position.**

Chapter 3: *Is Christ God?*

1. In what ways did Jesus Christ claim to be the Son of God (pp. 30-31)?

2. When we face the claims of Christ, there are four possible ways to explain his actions: he was a liar, a lunatic, a legend or the Son of God (pp. 32-33). What evidence exists to disprove that Jesus was a liar?

3. What evidence exists for or against the theory that Jesus was a lunatic?

4. Why might it be argued that the Gospels are accounts of an actual person, not a legend?

5. Many people claim that Jesus was a "great moral teacher" but not the Son of God. How would you answer such a person?

6. How did Jesus substantiate his claim to being God's Son (pp. 33-36)?

7. Reread the description of Jesus written by Bernard Ramm (p. 34). What aspect of his character would you find most comforting to have in a best friend?

8. What aspect you would like to emulate most? How can you begin to develop this more?

9. Take time now to add any new insights to your list of reasons for putting your hope in God through Christ Jesus.

> **Jesus Christ himself was the way to God. He was not merely a theological map to heaven.**

Chapter 4: *Did Christ Rise from the Dead?*

1. Read 1 Corinthians 15:3-28. The apostle Paul says in these verses that the resurrection of Jesus Christ is "of first importance" (v. 3) for proof of Christ's deity, the reversal of Adam's sin that resulted in death and assurance of our eternal life. How did Christ's resurrection accomplish these things?

2. Paul Little points out how the Christian church, the Christian sabbath and the Christian Scriptures were changed by Jesus' resurrection (pp. 38-39). How would your life be different if Jesus had never risen from the dead?

3. Read Matthew 28:11-15. Even Jesus' enemies admitted that his tomb was empty. The truth of Christ's resurrection rests on *how* the tomb was emptied. The authorities claimed that Jesus' followers removed the body. Given all that the disciples later endured to spread the word of Christ's resurrection, how likely does the author think this is (pp. 39-40)?

4. Other explanations often given are that the authorities moved the body or the disciples returned to the wrong tomb (p. 40). What makes these answers reasonable or unreasonable?

5. A more recent explanation suggests Jesus never really died but instead merely fainted (pp. 40-41). What makes this theory plausible? What loose ends would this theory leave?

6. At the time the New Testament books were written, there were still many alive who claimed to have seen Jesus alive again after his execution. Three explanations are that the people lied, hallucinated or indeed saw him (pp. 42-45). What evidence confirms or denies each of these?

7. Some of the greatest proofs of Jesus' resurrection are (1) the difficulty Jesus had in convincing his followers he was again alive; and (2) how the news changed them from fearful fugitives to bold, aggressive witnesses. How has your life been changed by belief in the resurrection?

8. Is there some way you would like to act on your belief in Christ's claims and power?

9. Take time now to add any new insights to your list of reasons for putting your hope in God through Jesus Christ.

> **We were created to communicate to a living and caring God . . . not to a stone idol.**

Chapter 5: *Is the Bible God's Word?*

1. Paul Little maintains that for the purpose of introducing a non-Christian to Jesus Christ and his claims, it is necessary only to prove that the Bible is made up of reliable historical documents (p. 47-48). Did you believe the Bible was *inspired* before you became a Christian or did you just think it was *reliable?* Explain. How could you focus conversation with non-Christians on Christ's claims instead of their view of the Bible?

2. According to the scriptural use of the word *inspired*, how is the Bible's inspiration different from the inspiration of Shakespeare's plays?

3. How does Jesus' own view of the Old Testament Scriptures and of the prophetic powers of John the Baptist support the inspiration of the Bible?

4. Jesus demonstrated that he believed the Old Testament was God's Word. In what ways do you act on your belief that the Bible is God's Word?

5. Often when nonbelievers claim that Christians take the Bible too literally, what do they mean (pp. 52-54)? Is this ever really a stumbling block for you? Why or why not?

148

Reading the Bible with understanding is like eating peanuts; the more you eat, the more you want to eat.

6. The author suggests that a clear definition of *inerrancy* is needed (p. 53). How would you define the term?

7. Fulfilled prophecy both validates the authenticity of the Old Testament documents and helps to prove Christ's claims (pp. 55-57). Would you use such an argument with one type of person more than another? Explain.

8. Consider the author's statement, "The confirmation of the Holy Spirit is what finally turns doubt into belief that the Bible is the Word of God" (p. 57). If you have experienced this, what was this experience like for you? How does this affect your Christian life?

9. Practically speaking, why is it important to determine if the Bible is God's Word, his letter to the world?

10. What can we expect of a letter from God that we could not expect of any other manuscript?

11. Are there any ways you need to redirect your thinking in order to take the Bible the way God intends it?

12. Take time now to add any new insights to your list of reasons for putting your hope in God through Christ Jesus.

Chapter 6: *Are the Bible Documents Reliable?*

1. The earliest existing manuscript of Caesar's *Gallic War* was copied nine hundred years after Caesar's time—five hundred years more than the gap between the earliest complete New Testament and its original texts. Why do historians accept the reliability of Caesar's *Gallic War* while the average person questions the reliability of the Bible?

2. How do the Dead Sea Scrolls and multiple versions of Scripture (pp. 61-63) help historians say, with R. Laird Harris, "Indeed, it would be rash skepticism that would now deny that we have our Old Testament in a form very close to that used by Ezra when he taught the law to those who had returned from the Babylonian captivity"?

3. A second problem in determining the Old Testament's reliability is determining which books rightly belong in the canon (pp. 66-69). What light does Christ's use of Old Testament Scripture shed on the Old Testament's authenticity?

The words between the covers of the Bible are God's thoughts. Approach with care.

4. Problems in New Testament reliability do not rest on lack of early manuscripts. However, we do not have Christ's "stamp of acceptance" on the books we include in the canon because they were written after his ascension (p. 68-69). What is the evidence in favor of the reliability of New Testament books?

5. Which questions concerning the reliability of the Bible seem more troublesome to you or people you know? Why?

6. Which answers offered in this chapter help resolve questions for you? What questions still remain unanswered in your mind?

7. If you have unanswered questions that seem important enough to pursue further, where could you go for help resolving them?

8. Take time now to add any new insights to your list of reasons for putting your hope in God through Christ Jesus.

Chapter 7: *Does Archaeology Verify Scripture?*

1. Of the archaeological findings mentioned in this chapter, which did you find to be most interesting and impressive? Explain your answer.

2. It stands to reason that if the Bible is true, archaeology could only substantiate biblical claims. Why were Christians once fearful of the archaeologist's pick?

3. When do archaeologists find "errors" in the biblical accounts (p. 72-73)?

4. As far as proving the Bible's accuracy, what are the limitations of archaeology (p. 72-73)?

5. What does it do to your faith to hear that archaeology substantiates Scripture?

6. When talking to a nonbeliever about the claims of Christ, would you mention archaeological findings that concern Scripture? Why or why not?

7. Some years ago, a rumor was widely published that scientists had proven that the earth had stopped its rotation for a day—the same amount of time that Joshua 10 tells us Joshua asked God to extend daylight so Israel could fight a key battle. The rumor turned out to be wishful thinking, but it showed people's desire to prove the *supernatural* aspects of Scripture. Do you ever have this desire? Why or why not?

8. Do you think such evidence would really make a difference to those who do not yet believe?

9. Take time now to add any new insights to your list of reasons for putting your hope in God through Jesus Christ.

Archaeology impressively confirms God's meticulous preservation of his message for all humankind.

150

Chapter 8: *Are Miracles Possible?*

1. Think back. When you have read of Christ's miracles in the Gospels, what reactions have you had?

2. What do we mean by *natural law* or the *laws of nature* (p. 87)?

3. Is God ruled by the laws of nature? Explain.

4. What is the relationship between the laws of nature and miracles (pp. 88-89)?

5. Some health authorities believe 85 percent of all illnesses is psychosomatic. Do you believe Christ healed only psychosomatic illnesses when he was on earth? Explain.

6. What two purposes did biblical miracles fulfill (pp. 88-89)?

7. The chapter contends that having the complete revelation of God in the Bible, we no longer need new miracles performed for our own science-oriented generation (p. 90). Do you agree with this? Why or why not?

8. Do you believe having the Bible to read fulfills the second purpose of miracles, "to demonstrate God's love by relieving suffering"? Why or why not?

9. Besides miracles, in what ways does God use his people to accomplish God's purposes of confirming faith and demonstrating God's love by relieving suffering?

10. How can you tell the difference between biblical miracles and "pagan" miracles (p. 91-92)?

Jesus was himself the one convincing permanent miracle.

11. What reasons have been offered for dismissing the disciples' testimony concerning the miracles Christ performed (pp. 93-94)?

12. How valid do you think these criticisms are?

13. Many times when a person expresses doubts about miracles or prophecy, the person has a deeper problem underneath. How can you get to the root cause of the disbelief?

14. Take time now to add any new insights to your list of reasons for putting your hope in God through Christ Jesus.

Chapter 9: *Do Science & Scripture Agree?*

1. What can happen when authorities, such as Bible scholars or scientists, make assumptions beyond the scope of their discipline (pp. 96-97)?

2. What would you say is the difference between *science* and *scientism?* What are some examples?

3. How have well-meaning Jews or Christians "added to the Word of God"?

4. Why do we limit the controversy between science and Scripture by "sticking to the facts"? What "facts" are valid to discuss?

5. Paul Little cautions against two extremes Christians should avoid in viewing evolution: (1) that evolution has been proven without a doubt; (2) that evolution is only a theory with little evidence behind it (p. 111). How has evolution been presented to you in the past in secular and Christian settings?

6. After reading this chapter, how do you view evolution and creationism?

7. Think about a friend who believes in evolution. How would you steer the conversation away from a scientific debate to a discussion of Christ and his claims?

8. Can you think of ways you have assumed that science must be "wrong" out of fear that it contradicts Scripture? If so, what are they? What do you think now?

9. If you have been skeptical about science for fear it contradicted what a Christian should believe, what are some ways you could open up to science without compromising your Christ-centered presuppositions?

10. Take time now to add any new insights to your list of reasons for putting your hope in God through Christ Jesus.

> **The brilliant system of the sun, planets and comets could only proceed from the counsel and domain of an intelligent, powerful Being.**

151

Chapter 10: *Why Does God Allow Suffering & Evil?*

1. In what instances do people lay blame unjustly on God for suffering and evil?

2. Can you think of any occasions when God was responsible for evil or suffering in Scripture, history or recent events? If so, what are some?

3. What would happen to the world we know if God completely stamped out evil (p. 114-15)? What prevents God from *occasionally* intervening in human affairs to combat evil or relieve suffering?

4. How has God already demonstrated that he wants to rid the world of suffering and evil (pp. 116-17)?

5. Do you see God doing this today? Would prayer cause him to do this more?

6. Would you prefer a world in which people were always rewarded for good and punished for evil (pp. 116-17)? Why or why not?

7. Scripture tells us that sometimes God rewards good and warns about and then punishes evil. How have you seen this in daily life?

8. Where is God when his creation suffers (pp.119-20)?

9. The question of why God allows suffering and evil goes beyond *why* we believe in God to *what* we will believe about him. How does the answer to this question affect our Christian life?

10. "The same sun melts the butter and hardens the clay" (p. 122). Is there someone you know who seems to be like clay but is turning into butter? How can you represent Christ to that person?

11. In your own experience, has suffering brought you closer to God or alienated you from him?

12. If Christ were standing beside you, what would you tell him about your suffering or the injustice you see? What would you ask?

13. Take time now to add any new insights to your list of reasons for putting your hope in God through Christ Jesus.

> "Everything of value I've ever learned in life has been through suffering."
>
> *Malcolm Muggeridge*

Chapter 11: *Does Christianity Differ from Other World Religions?*

1. Many people believe that all religions worship the same God but call that God by different names. To refute this claim Paul Little briefly outlines four world religions—Buddhism, Hinduism, Islam and Christianity (pp. 128-33). Take time to summarize the chief points of each religion, including the religion's ultimate goal, method of achieving that goal and concept of a deity.

2. What are the greatest similarities between Christianity and these other religions? the greatest differences (pp. 129-34)?

3. Taking these points into account, what is the value of comparing religions to see which is better (provides assurance of salvation, has done most for society, offers a palatable explanation for evil in the world, and so on)?

4. Should such comparisons affect how a person chooses a religion? defends a religion? Explain.

5. The author states, "In a conversation with the Jewish religious leaders, Jesus discussed [whether God was Jesus' Father]. 'God is our Father,' they said. Jesus said to them, . . . 'You do not belong to God' (John 8:47). . . . It is quite obvious the Jewish leaders were not sincere seekers. If people are seeking the true God, their sincerity will be evident" (p. 133). Is sincerity the only prerequisite for being able to accept Christ? Explain.

6. What types of healing may need to take place before you or some sincere seekers will find Christ or trust him fully?

7. Take time now to add any new insights to your list of reasons for putting your hope in God through Christ Jesus.

> If it's the true way, one way is not narrow.

Chapter 12: *Is Christian Experience Valid?*

1. What are common ways non-Christians rationalize away the Christian experience (pp. 135-36)?

"**Measure all my accomplishments, add them all together, and they are nothing compared to the living water Jesus Christ offers to the thirsty.**"

Malcolm Muggeridge

"**Come to me, all you who are weary and burdened, and I will give you rest.**"

Jesus Christ

2. What is the "common-factor fallacy" (p. 136)?

3. In recent years, how have society and the media used it to discredit the Christian experience?

4. Christians often use these same presuppositions to understand people of other religions. Why is this so?

5. Could one hundred atheists be found whose lives have been changed for the better by atheism (p. 139)? Is this a valid argument for or against atheism? Why?

6. What gives the Christian experience greater validity than the person in Paul Little's example who believes the fried egg on his ear has brought him joy, peace, purpose in life, forgiveness of sins and strength for living (pp. 139)?

7. What would you say to the person who sincerely accepts Christ as Savior and Lord but doesn't feel the joy, peace, purpose in life, forgiveness of sins and strength for living that should accompany a Christian conversion experience?

8. Do you know someone who was drawn to Christ not because of the intellectual evidence for Christ but because Christianity seemed to benefit the lives of others? What Scripture passages would negate or validate this way to meet Christ?

9. How could you effectively present some of the truths in this chapter to a person who thinks your Christian experience is a fantasy?

10. Take time now to add any new insights to your list of reasons for putting your hope in God through Christ Jesus.

153

NOTES

Chapter 1: *Is Christianity Rational?*

1. C. S. Lewis, *Mere Christianity* (New York: Macmillan, 1943), p. 24.

2. R. C. Sproul, *Knowing Scripture* (Downers Grove, Ill.: InterVarsity Press, 1977), p. 17.

3. Antony Flew, "Theology and Falsification," in *New Essays in Philosophical Theology,* ed. Antony Flew and Alasdair MacIntyre (London: SCM Press, 1955), n.p.

4. On the issue of theological verification, see John W. Montgomery, "Inspiration and Inerrancy: A New Departure," *Evangelical Theological Society Bulletin* 8 (spring 1956): 45-75.

5. Bill Hybels, *The God You're Looking For* (Nashville: Thomas Nelson, 1997), p. 7.

6. Stephen Hawking, *A Brief History of Time* (New York: Bantam, 1988), p.175.

7. C. S. Lewis, *The Quotable Lewis* (Wheaton, Ill.: Tyndale House, 1989), p.229.

8. C. S. Lewis, *God in the Dock* (Grand Rapids, Mich.: Eerdmans, 1970), pp. 108-9.

Chapter 2: *Is There a God?*

1. Mortimer Adler, *Great Books of the Western World,* ed. Robert Maynard Hutchins, vol. 2 (Chicago: Encyclopaedia Britannica, 1952), p. 561.

2. Samuel Zwemer, *The Origin of Religion* (Neptune, N.J.: Loizeaux Bros., 1945), n.p.

3. R. C. Sproul, *Reason to Believe* (Grand Rapids, Mich.: Zondervan, 1978), p.112.

4. Lincoln Barnett, *The Universe and Dr. Einstein* (New York: Bantam, 1974), p. 95.

5. Sir Fred Hoyle, *The Intelligent Universe* (London: Michael Joseph, 1983), pp.11-12, 19, 251.

6. Robert Grange, *Origins and Destiny* (Waco, Tex.: Word, 1986), p. 39.

7. Bernard Ramm, *The Christian View of Science and Scripture* (Grand Rapids, Mich.: Eerdmans, 1954), p. 148.

8. R. E. D. Clark, *Creation* (London: Tyndale Press, 1946), p. 20.

9. Pattle P. Pun, *Evolution: Nature and Scripture in Conflict?* (Grand Rapids, Mich.: Zondervan, 1982), p. 226.

10. Richard Lewontin, "Adaptation," *Scientific American* 239, no. 3:212.

11. James Brooks, *Origins of Life* (Belleville, Mich.: Lion, 1985), pp. 109-10.

12. Robert Jastrow, *God and the Astronomers* (New York: W. W. Norton, 1978), pp. 12-14, 116.

13. William Lane Craig, *The Existence of God and the Beginning of the Universe* (San Bernardino, Calif.: Here's Life, 1979), pp. 59-60.

14. Jastrow, *God and the Astronomers,* pp. 11, 14, 113-14.

15. C. S. Lewis, *Mere Christianity* (New York: Macmillan, 1943), pp. 3, 11, 15-19.

Chapter 3: *Is Christ God?*

1. John R. W. Stott, *Basic Christianity* (Downers Grove, Ill.: InterVarsity Press, 1958), p. 26.

2. C. S. Lewis, "Miracles," quoted in Stott, *Basic Christianity,* p. 32.

3. Bernard Ramm, *Protestant Christian Evidences* (Chicago: Moody Press, 1953), p. 177.

4. Ibid.

Chapter 4: *Did Christ Rise from the Dead?*

1. David Strauss, *The Life of Jesus for the People,* 2nd ed. (London, 1879), 1:412.

2. B. F. Westcott, *The Gospel of the Resurrection,* 4th ed. (London, 1879), pp.4-6.

Chapter 5: *Is the Bible God's Word?*

1. Malcolm Muggeridge, *Jesus, the Man Who Lives* (New York: Harper & Row, 1975), p. 9.

2. J. D. Douglas, *New Bible Dictionary* (Downers Grove, Ill.: InterVarsity Press, 1962), p. 1259.

3. B. B. Warfield, *The Inspiration and Authority of the Bible* (New York: Oxford University Press, 1927), pp. 299ff.

4. Gordon Clark, ed., *Can I Trust My Bible?* (Chicago: Moody Press, 1963), pp.15-16.

5. E. J. Carnell, *An Introduction to Christian Apologetics* (Grand Rapids, Mich.: Eerdmans, 1950), p. 208.

6. Andrew E. Hill and John H. Walton, *A Survey of the Old Testament* (Grand Rapids: Mich.: Zondervan, 1991), p. 437.

7. Clark, *Can I Trust,* p. 27.

Chapter 6: *Are the Bible Documents Reliable?*

1. Andrew E. Hill and John H. Walton, *A Survey of the Old Testament* (Grand Rapids, Mich.: Zondervan, 1991), p. 14.

2. R. Laird Harris, "How Reliable Is the Old Testament Text?" in *Can I Trust My Bible?* ed. Gordon Clark (Chicago: Moody Press, 1963), p. 124.

3. Ibid., pp. 129-30.

4. B. F. Westcott and F. J. A. Hort, eds., *New Testament in Original Greek,* vol. 2 (London, 1881), p. 2.

5. Lee Strobel interviewing Bruce Metzger, in Strobel, *The Case for Christ* (Grand Rapids, Mich.: Zondervan, 1998), p. 63.

6. F. F. Bruce, *The New Testament Documents: Are They Reliable?* (Grand Rapids, Mich.: Eerdmans, 1959), pp. 12-13. Contains a full discussion of the dating of documents.

7. Ibid., p. 14.

8. F. F. Bruce, *The Books and the Parchments* (Westwood, N.J.: Revell, 1963), p. 178.

9. K. A. Kitchen, *The Bible and Its World* (Downers Grove, Ill.: InterVarsity Press, 1977), p. 131.

10. Bruce, *New Testament Documents,* p. 19.

11. Sir Frederic Kenyon, "The Bible and Archaeology," quoted in Bruce, *New Testament Documents,* p. 20.

12. E. J. Young, "The Canon of the Old Testament," in *Revelation and the Bible,* ed. C. F. Henry (Grand Rapids, Mich.: Baker, 1956), p. 156.

Chapter 7: *Does Archaeology Verify Scripture?*

1. W. F. Albright, "Archaeology and the Religion of Israel," in *An Introduction to Bible Archaeology,* ed. Howard F. Vos (Chicago: Moody Press, n.d.), p.121.

2. Millar Burrows, "What Mean These Stones?" in *An Introduction to Bible Archaeology,* ed. Howard F. Vos (Chicago: Moody Press, n.d.), pp. 91-92.

3. H. Darrell Lance, *The Old Testament and the Archaeologist* (Philadelphia: Fortress, 1981), p. 65.

4. Leighton Ford, *The Power of Story* (Colorado Springs: NavPress, 1994), p. 13.

5. A. R. Millard, *The Bible B.C.* (Phillipsburg, N.J.: Presbyterian & Reformed, 1982), p. 9.

6. A. Rendle Short, *Modern Discovery and the Bible* (London: Inter-Varsity, 1949), p. 137.

7. Millard, *Bible B.C.,* p. 51.

8. A. R. Millard, *Treasures from Bible Times* (Belleville, Mich.: Lion, 1985), pp.54-57.

9. Edwin M. Yamauchi, *The Stones and the Scripture* (New York: Lippencott, 1972), p. 38.

10. Ibid., p. 39.

11. Millard, *Treasures from Bible Times,* pp. 47-48.

12. Yigael Yadin, quoted in Yamauchi, *Stones,* p. 68.

13. Millard, *Bible B.C.,* p. 25.

14. Ibid., p. 27.

15. Short, *Modern Discovery,* p. 184.

16. R. F. Dougherty, quoted in Millard, *Bible B.C.,* p. 29.

17. F. F. Bruce, "Archaeological Confirmation of the New Testament," in *Revelation and the Bible,* ed. C. F. Henry (Grand Rapids, Mich.: Baker, 1958), p.320.

18. Ibid., p. 323.

19. Ibid., p. 324.

20. Ibid., p. 327.

21. Keith N. Schoville, *Biblical Archaeology in Focus* (Grand Rapids, Mich.: Baker, 1978), p. 156.

Chapter 8: *Are Miracles Possible?*

1. J. N. Hawthorne, *Questions of Science and Faith* (London: Tyndale Press, 1960), p. 55.

2. Bernard Ramm, *Protestant Christian Evidences* (Chicago: Moody Press, 1953), p. 140.

3. Ibid., pp. 140-41.

4. Ibid., pp. 142-43.

5. C. S. Lewis, "Miracles," quoted in Ramm, *Protestant Christian Evidences,* p.143.

6. Ramm, *Protestant Christian Evidences,* p. 160.

7. Ibid., p. 40.

8. G. K. Chesterton, *The Quotable Chesterton* (Garden City, N.Y.: 1987), p. 218.

156

Chapter 9: *Do Science & Scripture Agree?*

1. *U. S. News & World Report,* December 1, 1980, p. 62.

2. Quoted in *Christianity Today,* October 8, 1982, p. 38.

3. J. P. Moreland, *The Creation Hypothesis* (Downers Grove, Ill.: InterVarsity Press, 1994), p. 17.

4. J. N. Hawthorne, *Questions of Science and Faith* (London: Tyndale Press, 1960), p. 4.

5. Hugh Ross, *The Creator and the Cosmos* (Colorado Springs: NavPress, 1993), p. 105.

6. Phillip Johnson, *Defeating Darwinism by Opening Minds* (Downers Grove, Ill.: InterVarsity Press, 1997), pp. 68, 69. Richard Dawkins, one of today's most influential biologists, describes the evolutionist's creed as the "selfish gene."

7. Ross, *Creator and the Cosmos,* p. 107. Here again Dawkins shows the atheist's presupposition that the existence of an infinite Designer is unthinkable.

8. Johnson, *Defeating Darwinism,* p. 76.

9. Moreland, *Creation Hypothesis,* p. 205.

10. Johnson, *Defeating Darwinism,* p. 77.

11. G. A. Kerkut, *The Implications of Evolution* (London: Pergamon, 1960), p.20.

12. The biblical account describes God as creating the living creatures, the birds that fly and the creatures of the sea using the phrase "according to their kinds." It is logical to ask if the word *kind* is the same as *species* (Genesis 1:21, 24). Kenneth Kantzer, author and theologian, answers that it is not.

It is "simply 'kind' in a most general way, and could apply to anything from a Linnean phylum to a Linnean species. It is even pressing too much into the phrase 'after its kind' to interpret it to mean that God individually created each 'kind' by a separate act . . . [but] each kind reproduces offspring like itself" (Kenneth S. Kantzer, "Guideposts for the Current Debate over Origins," *Christianity Today,* October 8, 1982, pp. 23, 26).

13. A. E. Wilder-Smith, *The Natural Sciences Know Nothing of Evolution* (San Diego: Master Books, 1981), p. 131.

14. Johnson, *Defeating Darwinism,* p. 16.

15. Ross, *Creator and the Cosmos,* pp. 19-20.

16. Ibid., p. 73.

17. Ross, *Creator and the Cosmos,* pp. 118-21.

18. Francis A. Schaeffer, *No Final Conflict* (Downers Grove, Ill.: InterVarsity Press, 1975), p. 16.

19. Davis A. Young, "An Ancient Earth Is Not a Problem; Evolutionary Man Is," *Christianity Today,* October 8, 1982, p. 42.

20. Kantzer, "Guideposts for the Current Debate," p. 26.

21. W. A. Criswell, *The Bible for Today's World* (Grand Rapids, Mich.: Zondervan, 1966), p. 30.

22. Kerkut, *Implications of Evolution,* p. 3.

23. J. P. Moreland, Seeds Resource Audio (South Barrington, Ill.: Willow Creek Community Church, 1998).

Chapter 10: *Why Does God Allow Suffering & Evil?*

1. Hugh Evan Hopkins, *Mystery of Suffering* (Downers Grove, Ill.: InterVarsity Press, 1959).

2. Ibid., p. 13.

3. J. B. Phillips, *God Our Contemporary* (New York: Macmillan, 1960), pp.88-89.

Chapter 11: *Does Christianity Differ from Other World Religions?*

1. *Open Doors,* 1996-1997 (Annapolis Junction, Md.: Institute of International Education, 1997).

2. Ravi Zacharias, *Can Man Live Without God* (Dallas: Word, 1994), pp.126-31.

3. Bill Hybels and Mark Mittelberg, *Becoming a Contageous Christian* (Grand Rapids, Mich.: Zondervan, 1994), p. 151.

4. Ibid., p. 155.

5. William Lane Craig, *No Easy Answers* (Chicago, Ill.: Moody Press, 1990), p.102.

Chapter 12: *Is Christian Experience Valid?*

1. Anthony Standen, *Science Is a Sacred Cow* (New York: E. P. Dutton, 1962), p. 25.

2. Orville S. Walters, *You Can Win Others* (Winona Lake, Ind.: Light & Life, 1950), n.p.

3. D. Martyn Lloyd-Jones, *Conversions: Psychological or Spiritual* (Downers Grove, Ill.: InterVarsity Press, 1959), p. 13.

4. J. B. Phillips, *God Our Contemporary* (New York: Macmillan, 1960), pp.22-23.

5. Ravi Zacharias, *Can Man Live Without God* (Dallas: Word, 1994), p.141

The Word at Work Around the World

A vital part of Cook Communications Ministries is our international outreach, Cook Communications Ministries International (CCMI). Your purchase of this book, and of other books and Christian-growth products from Cook, enables CCMI to provide Bibles and Christian literature to people in more than 150 languages in 65 countries.

Cook Communications Ministries is a not-for-profit, self-supporting organization. Revenues from sales of our books, Bible curricula, and other church and home products not only fund our U.S. ministry, but also fund our CCMI ministry around the world. One hundred percent of donations to CCMI go to our international literature programs.

CCMI reaches out internationally in three ways:

· Our premier International Christian Publishing Institute (ICPI) trains leaders from nationally led publishing houses around the world.

· We provide literature for pastors, evangelists, and Christian workers in their national language.

· We reach people at risk—refugees, AIDS victims, street children, and famine victims—with God's Word.

Word Power, God's Power

Faith Kidz, RiverOak, Honor, Life Journey, Victor, NexGen — every time you purchase a book produced by Cook Communications Ministries, you not only meet a vital personal need in your life or in the life of someone you love, but you're also a part of ministering to José in Colombia, Humberto in Chile, Gousa in India, or Lidiane in Brazil. You help make it possible for a pastor in China, a child in Peru, or a mother in West Africa to enjoy a life-changing book. And because you helped, children and adults around the world are learning God's Word and walking in his ways.

Thank you for your partnership in helping to disciple the world. May God bless you with the power of his Word in your life.

For more information about our international ministries, visit www.ccmi.org.

Additional copies of this and
other Victor books are available wherever
good books are sold.

If you have enjoyed this book,
or if it has had an impact on your life,
we would like to hear from you.

Please contact us at:

VICTOR BOOKS
Cook Communications Ministries, Dept. 201
4050 Lee Vance View
Colorado Springs, CO 80918
Or visit our Web site:
www.cookministries.com

Victor®

The Bible Teacher's Teacher